How to Start, Run, and Grow a Reputable & Profitable

Pawnshop Business

Become a Successful Pawnbroker: Learn How to Deal in Gold, Silver, Jewelry, Antiques, Guns, Collectibles & Electronics

By

Carl Eddlemon

Copyright © 2020 – **Streets of Dream Press**

All Rights Reserved.

No part of this publication may be reproduced, stored in a retrieval system or transmitted in any form or by any means, electronic, mechanical, photocopying, recording or otherwise without the proper written consent of the copyright holder, except brief quotations used in a review.

Published by:

Streets of Dream Press

Cover & Interior designed

By

Robin Albright

First Edition

Contents

Introduction 12
   History of Pawnbroking 13
      The Early Days of Pawning 13
      The Modern Pawnshop 15
What is a Pawnbroker? 17
   How the Pawn Process Works 19
   Types of Transactions You Can Do 20
What You Need to Know 22
   Communicating with the Public 23
   Knowledge of Items 23
   Business Knowledge 24
   Be Aware of the Laws 24
   Business Licensing 24
Establishing a Pawnshop 26
   Location 28
   Certificate of Occupancy 29
   Security Concerns 30
      Video Surveillance 31
      Security Services 31

- Governing Laws 33
  - Federal Laws 33
  - State Laws 34
- Pawnshop Business Plan 37
  - Five Things to Do Before Writing a Business Plan 37
    - Define a Purpose 38
    - Develop Your Vision 38
    - Have a Clear Business Model 39
    - Determine Your Target Market 39
    - Test Your Idea 39
  - Writing a Business Plan Step-by-Step 40
    - Executive Summary 41
    - Products and Services 42
    - Mission Statement 42
    - Vision Statement 42
    - Business Structure 43
    - Market Analysis 43
    - Sales and Marketing Strategy 44
    - Financial Projections 44
    - Sustainability and Expansion Strategy 45
  - Business Plan Advice 45

- Type of Business Structures 46
  - Sole Proprietorship 47
    - Who Should Choose It 47
    - How to Form 47
    - What You Need to Know 48
  - Partnership 49
    - Who Should Choose It 49
    - How to Form 50
    - What You Need to Know 50
  - Limited Liability Corporation (LLC) 52
    - Who Should Choose It 52
    - How to Form 53
    - What You Need to Know 53
  - Corporation 53
    - Who Should Choose It 54
    - How to Form 54
    - What You Need to Know 54
    - C Corporation 55
    - S Corporation 55
    - B Corporation 55
- Startup Costs 58

- Sample Budget 60
- Considerations 61

Insurance to Consider 65
- General Liability Insurance or Commercial Liability 65
  - What It Covers 65
  - Required 66
  - Cost 66
- Product Liability Insurance 66
  - What It Covers 66
  - Required 66
  - Cost 67
- Property Insurance 67
  - What It Covers 67
  - Required 67
  - Cost 67
- Sprinkler Leakage Insurance 67
  - What It Covers 68
  - Required 68
  - Cost 68
- Professional Liability Insurance or 'Errors and Omissions' or Malpractice Insurance 68

- What It Covers 68
- Required 69
- Cost 69

Umbrella Insurance 69
- What It Covers 69
- Required 69
- Cost 70

Worker's Compensation Insurance 70
- What It Covers 70
- Required 70
- Cost 70

Internet Business Insurance 71
- What It Covers 71
- Required 71
- Cost 71

Crime and Fidelity Insurance 71
- What It Covers 72
- Required 72
- Cost 72

Business Interruption Expense Insurance 72
- What It Covers 72

- Required 72
  - Cost 73
- Business Auto Insurance 73
  - What It Covers 73
  - Required 73
  - Cost 73
- Dealing with Merchandise 75
  - Merchandising 76
  - How to Source Merchandise 79
  - Dealing with Gold and Silver 83
  - Dealing with Guns 85
  - Dealing with Antiques and Collectibles 89
    - What to Know When Buying 90
    - How Professionals Value Antiques and Collectibles 91
    - Where to Find Value Online 91
    - Doing Offline Research 92
    - What to Know Before Selling 93
  - Dealing with Jewelry 94
- Staffing a Pawnshop 98
  - Hiring 98
  - Training 100

Retention 102

Promotion, Advertising, and Marketing 105

    Image Management 105

    Customer Relations and Customer Service 108

Inventory and POS Systems 117

How to Grow Your Pawnshop 120

    Displaying Electronics 121

    Firearms Tips 121

    Involve the Community 122

    Use Your Managers 123

    Take Care of Your Employees 124

    Maintain Your Store 125

    Improve Your Loan Game 125

    Improving Your Jewelry Game 126

    Improved Inventory Management 127

    Use Facebook 129

    Improve Sales 130

    Use Your Software 131

    Learn from the Competition 131

Conclusion 133

Appendix: State by State Requirements 134

Alabama 134

Alaska 134

Arkansas 135

Arizona 135

California 135

Colorado 136

Connecticut 136

District of Columbia 137

Delaware 137

Florida 137

Georgia 138

Hawaii 138

Iowa 139

Idaho 139

Illinois 139

Indiana 140

Kansas 140

Kentucky 141

Louisiana 141

Massachusetts 141

Maryland 142

Maine	142
Michigan	143
Minnesota	143
Missouri	143
Mississippi	144
Montana	144
North Carolina	144
North Dakota	145
Nebraska	145
New Hampshire	145
New Jersey	146
New Mexico	146
Nevada	147
New York	147
Ohio	147
Oklahoma	148
Oregon	148
Pennsylvania	149
Rhode Island	149
South Carolina	149
South Dakota	150

Tennessee 150

Texas 151

Utah 151

Virginia 151

Vermont 152

Washington 152

Wisconsin 152

West Virginia 153

Wyoming 153

Introduction

There are plenty of business opportunities if you are looking to start your own business. I've researched plenty of options. After considering the pros and cons of many, I settled on what I felt was the best option to open a pawnshop. This may sound like a unique and possibly odd business choice, but it is actually a sound business decision. I want to start by telling you about what I found when researching pawnbroking and how I got my shop started so you can enjoy the benefits of this business opportunity as well.

History of Pawnbroking

People often think of pawnshops as a more recent development, but the fact is that pawnbroking actually has a long history throughout the world. This is due to the fact that throughout history, people have always found themselves in a place where they need additional funds, fast. The best solution to this problem is to "pawn" personal items for a loan that covers the cast value of the item. Historically, pawnbrokers were responsible for giving out monetary loans in return for an item of value. Let's take a brief moment to look at the history of pawnbroking.

The Early Days of Pawning

The first pawnshops started in Ancient China nearly 3,000 years ago and were used as a way to give short-term credit to peasants. While some pawnbrokers operated by themselves, most businesses were eventually run through a store.

Pawnbroking continued through Ancient Greece and Rome, where they helped get small businesses off the ground. Then in the Middle Ages, the Catholic Church placed restrictions on interest, and this temporarily stopped the growth of pawnshops. In Europe, in the 14th and 15th centuries, these rules were relaxed as short-term credit became a necessary way to finance businesses and give assistance to the poor. At the time, some families became known as money-lending families such as the Lombards of England and the Medicis of Italy. A famous case of pawning was in 1388 when King Edward III of England pawned his jewels to the Lombards in order to pay for the war against France.

The term "pawn" comes from the Latin word "patinum," which means cloth or clothing. Among the working class, clothes have often been the most valuable thing they owned. While the majority of pawnshops are privately operated, some public shops were started in Europe in the 18th century as charitable funds by offering low-interest loans to the poor class to help reduce debt. A common way that the poor class made it through the week in the 19th century was to pawn clothes on Monday and then retrieve them on payday on Friday. Since those who needed assistance were often those on the fringe of society, protections were used to prevent people from pawning stolen goods. England established the Pawnbrokers Act of 1872, which started regulations that protected pawnbrokers who accidentally sold stolen goods. This same act also regulated the amount of interest that could be applied to pawned items and put guidelines in place for the pawnbroking industry that are still in effect today.

The Modern Pawnshop

Within the last 100 years, the number of pawnshops within the United States has dramatically increased. Pawnshops were one of only a few institutions in the Great Depression-era that provided cash as the banks started to fail, and people were getting rid of cherished and valuable items in order to pay debts. Today, pawnshops are still the main source for people who want to turn items into cash. The pawnshop is essentially a mini bank for those who don't have checking accounts while also being an exchange for people from all class backgrounds who want to buy and sell unique, rare, or collectible items.

Throughout history, pawnshops have often been criticized and stigmatized as preying on the poor with high-interest rates and low value of goods in order to make a profit. However, there are organizations like the National Pawnbrokers Association that was established in 1988 to maintain the industry as a viable option for those who need cash. Pawnshops are required to maintain clear regulations about the terms of their contracts and the amount of interest they can charge for cash loans. Pawned items are also registered in order to prevent stolen goods from being sold.

Pawnshops are actually a place where you can find history, antiques, jewelry, and other items that have often been handed down through generations. Owners may actually know the source of items or offer stories of where the items come from. There is a lot that goes into working as a pawnbroker, and the business isn't for everyone. To help you decide if this business venture is right for you, we should next consider just what a pawnbroker is and what they do while also considering what a typical day includes and the work environment.

What is a Pawnbroker?

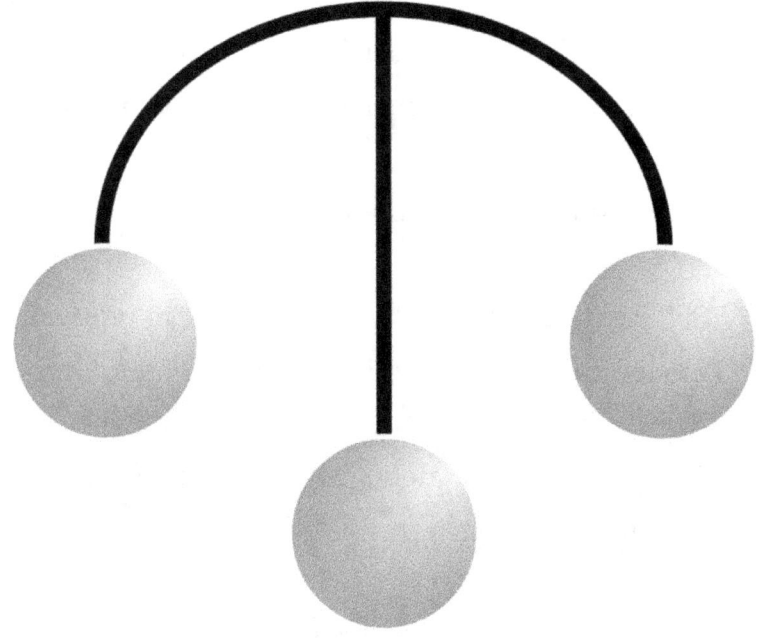

When you go to a pawnshop, you will hand over your item to a pawnbroker who will then value the item. The pawnbroker is an individual who is responsible for and performs the following roles:

- Estimating the value of items

- Examining electronics and tools to ensure they are functioning properly

- Weigh and inspect diamonds, gold and other jewelry for purity

- Reject items that don't meet specific condition requirements

- Negotiate loan amounts with customers based on the item value and how much cash the individual needs

- Sign contracts and disburse money

- Sell pawned items if the customers fail to return the money and interest within the period of the contract

- Ensure all appropriate registrations and licenses are maintained for the business

- Maintain all business records

- Supervise any employees

Most pawnbrokers work within a pawnshop and have normal business hours during the week. A typical day can include all of the above activities or very little based on the number of customers that come into the shop. In order to better understand how a day goes for a pawnbroker, we need to look at how the pawn process works.

How the Pawn Process Works

If a customer is in need of a small loan, they can bring an item of value to a pawnshop where a pawnbroker will appraise the resale value of the item using books and the internet. The average estimate for loans extended through a pawnshop is $70 to $100. The collateral or item can be repurchased by the customer for a fee or can allow the item to stay with the pawnbroker to be sold as a retail item.

Pawnbrokers will typically offer loans for 30-, 60- or 90-days, often based on the value of the item being offered as collateral. The loan amount is often about 40 percent less than the item value, with the industry average typically being about 33 percent. This means that if an item is valued at a retail amount of $150, then the loan offer will be $49.50.

The interest rate on a pawn loan will vary depending on the state since each state has its own interest rate cap. The range can be from 2 percent to 12 percent per month. Some pawnshops will also collect fees like stocking and handling fees in order to increase the profit margin. These fees can range from a low of 5 percent to as high as 20 percent a month. This means that a $50 loan in a 30-day period could end up costing a total of $3.50 to $16 in interest and fees on top of the loan amount.

Occasionally, customers will bring in an item to sell it outright rather than getting a loan in order to avoid paying interest or just because they no longer have a use for the item. In these cases, the pawnbroker will examine the item to determine the condition and then refer to books and the Internet to estimate the value of the item. The purchase offer will often be 40 percent less than the value of the item. So, if an item has a retail value of $100, then the pawnbroker will often offer to purchase the item for $35 to $40.

Pawnshops will also sell both purchased and collateral items like a normal retail store. Items are displayed on shelves or in windows. However, the items are sold differently in pawnshops since all items are negotiable in price. A pawnbroker will know the retail value and how much they paid for or loaned the item for; this is used to form the lowest acceptable price. This means that an item purchased for $100 with a retail value of $250 may be willing to accept as low as $200 for the item. Pawnshops are also a little different in terms of the items they buy and sell.

Types of Transactions You Can Do

As a pawnbroker, you'll want to turn a lot of property as fast as possible. The best chance of doing this is with smaller items that sell quickly. Some of the most common items a pawnbroker works with include the following:

- Appliances

- Jewelry

- Collectibles

- Coins

- Sporting Goods

- Tools

- Electronic Equipment

In addition to knowing what types of items you can pawn, there is some education and training that goes into becoming a pawnbroker. Most of it surrounds you with the valuing of items. Let's consider what you should know in order to be successful as a pawnbroker.

What You Need to Know

Pawnbrokers need to become a specialist in buying valuable merchandise, making loans with tangible collateral, and running a storefront operation to sell items.

This means you need to be well versed in appraising a range of items and in the art of negotiating sales and loans. Let's look at some specific things you need to learn.

Communicating with the Public

As a pawnbroker, you will be dealing with a range of personality types. People choose to pawn items for a range of reasons; some need the cash for other things, and others are simply looking to get rid of unwanted items.

As a pawnbroker, you need to communicate well with all types of customers; this includes explaining values and setting loan terms such as collateral and interest. While communicating, you need to be fair, calm, and able to rationally deal with customers who may be in dire circumstances.

Knowledge of Items

A pawnbroker also needs to be an appraiser and well-versed in determining authenticity. Having a background in appraising can be helpful, but you can also research items in order to determine fair market value.

This can be important when it comes to setting purchase prices and loan amounts. However, you'll also need to estimate how much of a profit you can make when reselling purchased items in the event they aren't claimed.

Business Knowledge

A successful pawnbroker will constantly evaluate the local marketplace in order to understand the state of the economy. If you overstock in one area such as jewelry, then you may find yourself with merchandise you can't move. You need to have a good sense of business as a pawnbroker, so you know what you are able to sell both online and in your store. This will help guide what merchandise you decide to take as collateral for a loan.

Be Aware of the Laws

Both state and federal laws influence the business of pawnbroking. These laws impact the sale, purchase, and pawning of firearms and potentially stolen merchandise. You need to work along with law enforcement as a pawnbroker and be knowledgeable on the practice of buying and holding items in order to track down and identify stolen items. You can visit the website of your secretary of state or contact the state's department of business and industry in order to get more information about specific regulations in your state.

Business Licensing

Before starting your business, you need to have a valid business license, and you may need to have additional licenses under your county or city regulations. One such license is the "privilege license" that is hard to obtain and often requires an extensive background search. Visit the small business administration website to determine what licensing requirements there are where you plan to open your pawnshop.

Now that we know about the job of a pawnbroker, if you are still interested in getting started in this field, let's move on to the next step. Let's look at the shop itself and what you need to open your storefront.

Establishing a Pawnshop

There are ten things you need to address first when establishing your new pawn shop:

1. Create a mission statement.

2. Clearly present your business.

3. Clearly define your finances.

4. Create a plan for customer service.

5. Investigate your retail space.

6. Choose a retail location with great customer traffic.

7. Create a well-defined store layout.

8. Legally establish your business.

9. Finalize the products you're offering.

10. Network with your potential customers.

A pawnshop is a place where anyone can buy and sell items. You can also use your valuables as collateral to get a loan for cash if you are in a bind and need some money right now. If a loan isn't repaid according to the terms set by the pawnbroker, then the item is put up for sale either at the pawnshop or online.

When it comes to setting up a pawnshop, there are four main things you want to consider:

- Where to locate your shop.
- Security concerns
- Governing laws in your state
- Rules and regulations

Let's consider each of these in greater detail, so you know what to expect when starting your pawnshop.

Location

The survival and growth of your pawnshop depend on you choosing the right location. If you aren't comfortable making this decision on your own, then you may want to speak with a consultant first. Choosing the wrong location for your pawnshop can have a negative impact on your business, and you may find it a struggle to make ends meet.

Pawnshops need to meet certain requirements when determining a location. For example, a pawnshop can only be located within a certain distance from establishments like schools. Before selecting a location for your pawnshop, you need to contact your city and county planning department for requirements. You can also choose to purchase an existing pawnshop if you don't want to go through the process of additional permits and zoning.

When choosing your ideal pawnshop location, you need to consider the following factors:

- Your mode of operation

- The demographics of the people near your location

- The amount of foot traffic in your area

- The availability of nearby competition both in pawnshops and other loan businesses

- Proximity to other businesses and services

- Accessibility and parking spaces for clients

- Ordinance and zoning restrictions

- Traffic and security issues

- The infrastructure of the building when it comes to the technology needed to run an online business and/or using electronic software

Certificate of Occupancy

Most pawnshops are often run from a storefront. If you are operating from a physical location, you'll need to get a Certificate of Occupancy or CO. The CO confirms that all building codes, zoning laws, and government regulations are met. What you need to know about a CO will depend on whether you are leasing a location or purchasing the building.

If leasing the location, it will often be the landlord's responsibility to get a CO. Before you lease a store, you should confirm with the landlord that they have or can get a valid CO that applies to a pawnshop. After any major renovations, a new CO will need to be issued. If you are going to renovate the building before opening your new pawnshop, then you need to include a clause in your lease agreement that lease payments won't start until a valid CO has been issued.

If you are going to purchase or build your pawnshop, then you will be responsible for getting your CO from the local authorities. To make sure you are in compliance and able to get a CO, you should ensure your location meets all building codes and zoning requirements. Before we look closer at these, let's consider one thing that you need to look at when choosing a location, and that is the security concerns.

Security Concerns

Pawnshops deal in high-value items and may often keep a lot of cash on hand. While a pawnshop can be a profitable business, this also means that you are susceptible to attempts of theft, break-ins, and robbery. So, if you are going to start a pawnshop, one thing you need to consider is how you are going to protect both yourself and your business. There are two main security options to consider.

Video Surveillance

It is important to have eyes on your business both inside and outside at all times. There should be no part of your business that isn't monitored and protected. This includes outside entrances and all the nooks in the back of the store. To do this, you need to install a good surveillance system both inside and outside. A surveillance system is good at deterring some would-be thieves. Even if it doesn't deter crimes, you'll at least have video evidence to prosecute crimes such as shoplifting. It will also help you have some peace of mind when you aren't physically at the store.

Security Services

If you are going to deal with higher value items such as jewelry, firearms, or original artwork, then you may want to invest in more security than just cameras. Consider hiring security services to protect your business. There are three main types of security services you can consider hiring for your business.

Drive-by security is something you can have both during open and closed hours. Often this form of security uses trained personnel and a marked security car to patrol your parking lot and the entrance areas. This type of security measure is often preventative since people are less likely to do something illegal when they know security can drive by at any potential time.

Another option you can consider is armed security, especially if you are dealing with high-end items such as jewelry, firearms, and antiques. This is a highly visible form of security that is also good if you have large amounts of cash on hand. Armed security allows you to make larger transactions during business hours, plus you can have an armed escort to your vehicle after closing hours or when making bank deposits. You can also hire unarmed security to stand by entries to keep an eye out on suspicious activity and react if needed. Many security guards are also trained in first aid in case it is needed.

Lastly, there is the option of a foot patrol. With this option, someone keeps an eye on your property by patrolling the interior and exterior areas both during the day and after hours. Foot patrol security can be dressed in uniform or can be dressed in traditional clothing to blend in with customer traffic.

No matter what option you choose, security officers sign an agreement with you. Under this agreement, you can have their either take action to remove individuals committing crimes, retain them for the police, or simply keep you aware of what is happening in your store. You can also choose to discuss your needs with a security company so they can offer advice on the best protection during all hours. Once you have addressed the security concerns for your pawnshop, you want to consider what governing laws apply to your business.

Governing Laws

When you choose to become a pawnbroker, you need to follow a number of federal, state, and local regulations. At the time of writing this, there are 13 regulations at the federal level alone. You don't have an option when it comes to following these regulations. There can be severe penalties if you knowingly or unknowingly fail to comply with these regulations. Consider just a few examples of the many state and federal laws you have to keep in mind when starting and running a pawnbroking business.

Federal Laws

The Truth in Lending Act (TILA) requires the disclosure of credit terms when performing consumer credit transactions. This means as a pawnbroker, you will need to explain clearly and in writing all the terms of your loans, including interest rates, fees, and other terms.

The Federal Trade Commission (FTC) has Safeguard and Privacy Rules regarding the protection of personal information such as name, address, phone number, and account information.

Federal firearm laws dictate record-keeping and background check requirements for both buyers and sellers of firearms.

The Internal Revenue Service has regulations on how you are to handle any cash transactions over $9,000.

State Laws

For most states, pawnbrokers need to get a license or register with a state agency such as the consumer protection agency or tax department. Take a look at the appendix at the back of this book for specific requirements by state.

Most states have a limit or cap for interest rates and fees when it comes to loans.

Pawnshops are often required to keep detailed records on anything bought or taken in as collateral. State regulations often require record keeping to include serial and model numbers, brand name, precious metal type, and gemstone description, among others.

In some states, there are also requirements for pawnshops to provide reports of purchases to the local police to help identify stolen goods. In other states, the pawnshop only has to honor a police request to check inventory for stolen goods or allow people with a police report to search inventory.

Most pawnshops need to be licensed at the state level, and others are only licensed at the local level, but a lot are licensed at both levels. You can't open a pawnshop without some form of licensing, and often there is more than one license involved. Depending on your location and what items you are going to handle, you may need things such as a pawnbroker's license, a precious metal dealer license, a secondhand dealer license, and a general business license.

Make sure you start the process early since most licenses will take time to obtain, and many also come with financial requirements. While this may seem restrictive or difficult, these requirements and regulations are in place to help your business be a success. If you can't afford to get all the regulations in place, then perhaps you'll need to change how you do business.

Where you choose to start your pawnshop will have an impact on the regulations you need to follow, and these will influence how you do business. Regulations will influence things like maximum finance charges, minimum holding times, pledge disposal, and many other things.

Once you know how regulations will affect your business, you'll also want to put together a services contract that you can use in the course of business. However, this is also something that may be regulated in your area, so you'll have to ensure you have a proper form. Now that you know what goes into starting a pawnshop let's consider how to get started. The most important first step to take is to have a strong business plan.

Pawnshop Business Plan

Perhaps the most important first step in starting a pawnshop is to have a strong and detailed business plan. Not only does a business plan help you when getting financing for your business, but it also provides you with a detailed roadmap for how you will start your business, market, and grow.

Five Things to Do Before Writing a Business Plan

There is a lot involved in starting a new business and being prepared for all the steps that can make the process easier. One of the best ways to increase your chances of being prepared for your business is to have a solid business plan.

The standard information and the technical aspects are easy to do, but the abstract part consists of things you need to figure out before you start to write your business plan. To have better success when writing this, you should do five things in preparation.

Define a Purpose

It is important to identify and describe your business' core values and purpose. Having a purpose helps provide your business with direction so you can make decisions at all levels based on which course of action to take.

Develop Your Vision

The key to a successful business is to have a clear vision of what the business is going to accomplish. To do this, you need to have three to five key strategies that will help you reach your goals. Along with this, you need to have a clear mission statement or the why of what your business is doing.

The second most important thing is your "value proposition" which defines what makes your business unique within your chosen marketplace and how you intend to make your business different from others.

Have a Clear Business Model

Having a clear financial business model is important when it comes to placing details in your formal business plan. This includes hiring, pricing, sales, cost of acquisition, expenses, and growth.

The business plan needs to be reviewed and updated as the business develops and grows, and to stay organized it is best to update it every week, or every two weeks if it is going slow at first.

Determine Your Target Market

This can be one of the more difficult steps. Ask yourself why you are opening your pawn shop where you chose to and who is interested in it. Then ask why you are attracted to this type of client. Make sure you have a clear definition of who you are dealing with.

Test Your Idea

You've likely already done this step, but if not, you need to get out and talk to experts, potential customers, or anyone within your target market to determine the viability of your pawn shop.

Simply writing your business plan isn't going to mean your business will be an automatic success, but it does help provide a map to how you'll get there. The more effort you put into writing your business plan, the easier it will be to track your progress and see which areas you still lack in, or which ones you can relax about.

Writing a Business Plan Step-by-Step

A business plan needs to have nine specific areas:

- Executive Summary

- Products and Services

- Mission Statement

- Vision Statement

- Business Structure

- Market Analysis

- Sales and Marketing Strategy

- Financial Projection

- Sustainability and Expansion Strategy

In each of the subsequent sections of your business plan, you can begin brainstorming how to write the information contained in the different parts by answering the questions of each section.

Executive Summary

This section is where you put in the summary of your business, what you plan to achieve, who the competition is, and where you plan to grow your business. This section of the business plan should be concise and short as you'll be getting into more details later. You would most likely write this part last, even if it is the first part of your plan. Be concise. Important readers, such as bank executives, don't have time to read a novel.

Products and Services

In this section, you'll want to go into greater detail on the products and services you'll be working with. Discuss what types of products you'll work with and how your loan services will work.

How do you plan on selling items that aren't re-claimed?

How do you plan to adhere to state laws?

How do you plan to turn a profit?

Mission Statement

What is your mission statement for your business?

How does it impact and/or what role does it play in the day to day operation of your business?

What are the beliefs and values of your business?

Vision Statement

What are the future plans for your business?

Do you plan to expand to new areas or just open to new products and services?

What about your company and business model will help lead this expansion?

Business Structure

What is the workforce structure of your business?

Who will have what role in the company?

What is the background of your leadership team, and how does it help further your business?

How do you plan to hire the right employees?

Market Analysis

Who is your target market?

Who is most likely to seek your services, and is this number expected to increase or decrease?

What do you plan to do to keep profit coming to your business should these numbers decrease?

What is the forecasted outlook for the industry and your area?

Sales and Marketing Strategy

What are the sales and marketing strategies of your business?

How do you plan to get customers in the door?

How do you plan to retain customers and create return business?

What marketing platforms will you use?

Financial Projections

This section may be best filled out by someone experienced in finances unless you are comfortable doing it yourself.

Based on research and providing charts and specific numbers, what are the financial projections for the company?

In your first four years of operations, what are your projected profits?

What might disrupt your financial plans?

Sustainability and Expansion Strategy

What factors will influence the growth and expansion of your business?

What actions do you need to take, and what financial requirements do you have for growth?

How do you plan to retain staff?

Business Plan Advice

This information comprises all the essentials that must be included in a business plan. You'll want to be very detailed and specific when writing your business plan. If you aren't comfortable with any areas of the plan, then you can consider hiring an expert to put together your business plan for you.

One thing you'll need to do to prepare for your business plan is determining how much startup capital you need. In order to do this, you need to understand what startup costs are associated with a pawnshop.

Type of Business Structures

Starting a business is fun, but a little overwhelming and certainly confusing if you are unsure as to what to do next. By this point, you have both a business and a financial plan. So, what now?

One of the more confusing areas is choosing a business structure. Even if you know the options, how can you know which is right for your pawn shop? In this chapter we are going to look at the types of business structures and how you can choose the right one for your preferences.

Sole Proprietorship

The business is entirely yours, and you will assume complete responsibility. This means you get all the profits but are also liable for all losses.

Who Should Choose It

When you choose to run your small business by yourself, you are going to be in charge of all the aspects involved in running the business.

If this is appealing to you, then a sole proprietorship may be a good option, so long as you understand the responsibilities involved and have a Plan B in case the business did not turn out the way you intended it to at first or may need modifications.

How to Form

This is one of the easiest business structures to form. In fact, there is no action required on your part to form this business structure. You will need to do some work for licensing and regulations depending on the industry your business is in, so you'll want to check with the local secretary of state about the necessary regulations.

In addition, if you are going to do business under a name that isn't your own, you'll need to file a DBA or Doing Business As.

What You Need to Know

While a sole proprietorship is basic and fairly simple, there are some things to consider:

1. A sole proprietorship is also known as a "pass-through" tax entity. This means that all profits and losses are passed through you as the business owner and you need to report them on your taxes. So, you'll need to file a Schedule C, Form 1040, and Schedule SE when filing your taxes.

2. While you can be the sole owner under a sole proprietorship, this doesn't mean you can't have employees. However, having employees will make your taxes slightly more complicated.

3. It can be more difficult to raise money with a sole proprietorship as well. This is because you won't be able to sell stock in your company and thus won't be

able to increase your company's wealth as quickly as other types of business structures.

4. Getting a bank loan as a sole proprietorship is also more problematic since you are less credible from the banks' point of view unless you have a solid financial backer.

5. Lastly, be aware that you are assuming full responsibility. If you can't pay your debts or if your business fails, then your personal assets are at risk. You will also be held liable if there are any legal issues, so the authorities can go after those personal assets and use them to pay off any investors.

Partnership

When you choose to partner with someone for your business you may choose to share ownership, so all parties involved have a share over input and participation in the company, this is still a simple business structure.

Who Should Choose It

This is a slightly bigger version of a sole proprietorship. It is best for when two or more people want to form an agreement and start a business together. The parties will be equal participants and bring their own unique viewpoints to the business.

How to Form

As with a sole proprietorship, doing business with someone basically forms the basis of a partnership. If you plan to do business other than your name or that of your partner, then you need to file a DBA.

Certain licenses or permits are also needed depending on your type of business and the state you operate in, so check with your local secretary of state office for specifics.

What You Need to Know

It is important to note that there are different types of partnership options. The type you choose will depend on how long you want to be partners and what active role each party is taking in the business.

General Partnership

Assumes all parties involved are involved equally: including all profits, liabilities, and duties. If anything is intentionally unequally split, then it needs to be noted in the official partnership agreement.

Limited Partnership

This format is often used when one partner serves in an investor role with limited input into the operations of the company. This format is more complex and typically isn't used as often unless the intention is to eventually become a sole proprietor.

Joint Venture

If you are planning to partner with someone for just one specific project, then the joint venture format is best. It is similar to a general partnership but is only for a specific period of time to complete a single project.

Before choosing a partnership, there are three things you need to consider, of course:

1. While not necessary, it is highly recommended that you outline a partnership agreement before starting a partnership. This will help ensure you start the business on the right foot and establish the limitations for both parties. It will allow you to clearly define what each person is responsible for and what will happen should you decide to quit working together.

2. Like a sole proprietorship, partnerships are also "pass-through" tax entities. This means all profits and losses are passed to the partner owners, so the risk and benefit factors are still the same, which is

something both people involved need to take in mind at all times.

3. Since you should have a lawyer review your partnership agreement, you'll want to take this added cost into account when calculating your startup costs.

Limited Liability Corporation (LLC)

With the two previous options, the scariest factor is that you'll be personally responsible if something goes wrong with the business and you or your partner may not be able to pay for the resulting costs.

The LLC structure offers you the best of everything. It gives you the flexibility of the previous two structures, but limits the responsibilities of those involved, like a corporate structure. This is also the most common type of business structure for most pawn shops.

Who Should Choose It

If you have assets that you want to protect without involving your business, an LLC is your best choice. It can also be a good option if you own a business within an industry that is prone to lawsuits so you can protect your personal assets.

How to Form

Forming an LLC is a little more difficult since you'll have to choose a compliant name, file articles of organization, and create an operating agreement. You'll also need to file for specific licenses or permits and a DBA if you need one.

What You Need to Know

While choosing an LLC has many advantages, it is a more complex structure, and you'll need to consider the following to determine if an LLC structure is right for you.

1. An LLC is considered a pass-through tax entity, like the two previous structures. However, under an LLC structure, you are only taxed on your share of the profits, which are filed under your personal taxes.

2. In almost all states except Massachusetts, you can form an LLC with a single individual. In some situations, starting an LLC can be a better option than starting a sole proprietorship.

Corporation

A corporation involves shareholders, a complex legal structure, and intricate tax requirements. It is what most people think of when they think of big business. While not uncommon, it is probably the more complex of all the options for a pawn shop owner.

Who Should Choose It

This is one of the most complicated business structures to handle, so you may not want to choose it if you are running the business yourself or just partnering with a few people unless you have prior experience in the field.

A corporation is often recommended for companies that are larger, more established, have many employees, intend to sell stock, scale quickly, have outside investors, or any combination of these.

How to Form

The first step in forming a corporation is to register your business name. You'll also need to file articles of incorporation and get a Federal Tax Identification number or EIN for that business as a separate entity.

What You Need to Know

It is important to know there are several types of corporate structures to choose from. The most common type is known as a C Corporation, or C Corp. There are also a few others you should know about before choosing this option. Let's look at all of them.

C Corporation

The most common type of corporation. All shareholders combine the funds and are then given stock in the business. From the standpoint of the IRS, a C Corp is a completely separate tax entity so that the company can take tax deductions.

Not to mention, profits are taxed twice; from the business standpoint and your personal taxes if you get income in the form of dividends. However, you can minimize this taxation with a good tax planning strategy.

S Corporation

The main difference between this structure and a C Corp is that profits and losses can be passed through to your personal tax return. In order to form an S Corp, you need to set up your business as a corporation first, then request S Corp status. It is best to speak with an attorney before starting this process, just to ensure you are well-informed on the benefits and risks involved.

B Corporation

If your business has a social mission or a good cause as its foundation, then you may want to consider this option. It is basically a C Corp that has been vetted and approved for B

Corp status. Some states give this form of the corporation a tax break.

While a corporation as a whole offers key advantages, it isn't the best option for everyone. There are a few things to keep in mind before choosing this option:

1. Since a corporation is its own entity, your personal assets are fully protected, so if worst comes to worst, you will not need to lose your personal assets such as a previously established business or a house.

2. A corporation has a greater chance of raising capital. All corporations can sell stock which will increase their ability to attract investors.

3. Since a corporation files taxes separately from personal taxes, your business will be eligible for additional tax breaks.

4. The biggest downside to a corporation is the fact that it is the most complicated structure. So be prepared to do a lot of work (typically involving a lawyer's assistance) to establish a solid corporation.

Depending on what your current income is, and how large you want your pawn shop to become, the structure or type of corporation you choose is bound to help you reach the next level in your endeavors. I personally suggest picking one with a realistic mindset.

Consulting with established pawn shop owners helps a great deal. Through this method, you find out the more intricate between-the-lines contexts of each structure and corporation, as well as the benefits and risks for each.

Startup Costs

Starting a pawnshop can cost as low as $10,000, but the actual number can also be much higher. A lot of it depends on your location and what type of pawnshop you want to start with. The income you are able to generate will come from the amount of money you are able to lend out, so this will also influence how much money you need to have when starting a pawnshop. If you want to deal with higher-end items, it makes sense that you'll want a larger amount of capital when starting a pawnshop.

Perhaps your largest fixed cost will be the rent for your shop space. Often it is best not to locate your pawnshop in a high-rent business district, but you should look for a location that is convenient for potential customers. You'll want to look for a space that gives you enough room for displaying, testing, and securely storing items.

The bulk of your cost and budget is going to come from operating capital. This is the money you need to have on hand in order to make loans and cover the costs of running your pawnshop.

You'll also want to make sure you have a budget to pay for security. As we've already discussed, pawnshops have often deal with a lot of valuable items and may even have a lot of cash on hand. This makes your business a target for thieves and having a good security system and/or security services is important for preventing loss and reducing the overall costs of your insurance coverage.

Insurance cost is another one to keep in your budget. You'll need comprehensive insurance in order to protect your business from loss and legal liability. The amount of insurance coverage a pawnshop needs will depend on the state where you are operating.

Another cost when starting a pawnshop is to have an initial inventory on hand. While you don't want to start with an extensive inventory, you also don't want an empty showroom when potential customers visit. You should have some inventory on hand before opening your pawnshop, but don't spend too much of your budget on it.

Lastly, you'll want to have a budget for a computer and software system. This will make it easier to keep records, print receipts, and research the value of items. Make sure you choose a computer system and software that meets your needs.

Sample Budget

150,000	Store build-out, signage, HVAC, restrooms, display cases, light fixtures, external lighting
5,000	Computers for office, office

	supplies, desks, chairs, printer, fax, phones
5,000	First year of insurance
75,000	First year of wages for employees
50,000	First year of rent at $4,000/month
10,000	First year marketing – fliers, commercials, coupons, business cards, and opening event
5,000	POS system and record-keeping software
300,000	Total

Considerations

The costs are determined by the size and location of your shop. Variables for your particular situation would be either increased or decreased wages, display fixtures, rent, and external improvements to the property.

If you were to purchase or lease an existing pawnshop, renovations for a similar layout might cost less because you are buying the build-out at your price. The rent, however, could be higher.

These decisions require the help of financial and accounting experts. If you are not an expert, you need help. What is not covered in the above are ongoing costs like utilities, trash, garbage, and appraisal services, if applicable.

Accommodations for these should be in your build-out, and, of course, necessary to open for business. Ongoing costs in your overhead will be part of your yearly operating costs and included in your business plan.

Renovating an existing pawnshop or retail space with a similar concept will cost less, while the rent may be comparatively higher because the value of the previous build-out is already in the purchase/rental price.

There are many economic factors that you must consider when you open a startup business. Economic factors that you must consider when starting retail pawnshop include, but are in no way limited to:

- Rent or lease payments

- Employee payroll

- Utility bill payments

- State, city, and local license fees

- Merchandising and inventory purchasing

- Legal counsel and retention

- Liability insurance

- Zoning law restrictions

- Music license (if you plan to play copyrighted music on public speakers in a place of business)

Do you have the economic means to pay monthly rent or lease payments for a place of business? It's a serious matter not to be taken lightly. The monthly rent for a retail store can cost you anywhere from several thousand to tens of thousands of dollars a month. Depending on your renting or lease agreement, such payments could be prone to unannounced increases as well.

For estimation's sake, the price to lease a small storefront in New Jersey or New York can cost you $70,000 to $85,000, respectively, and easily. But on the other hand, leasing a 1200-1500 SQF storefront in cities like Memphis, TN, or Louisville, KY may only cost you $3,000 to $4,000.

Do you plan to have any employees? When you are running a pawnshop, you have to keep track of inventory, how much money you are spending, how much revenue you are spending to pay, expenses, and keeping track of profits. There is a lot of work and meticulous bookkeeping involved with pawnshop ownership. Hiring one or two or more employees part-time or full-time at minimum wage will cost you tens of thousands of dollars per person annually.

How much you pay in utility payments will depend upon where you open your business and how many hours a day that you plan to stay open for operations. Count on it from being hundreds to thousands of dollars per month, if not more.

These figures might sound scary, and I hope they haven't given you sticker shock. Of course, any venture can be started more inexpensively or financed frugally if you do your research. There are many factors that influence how much you might need in your locale to begin a business like this. Your actual startup costs might be lower or higher than the example budget.

Insurance to Consider

When you start a pawn shop, the last thing you want to do is spend money for protection you don't need. However, ignoring important insurance can also have a major impact on your ability to function as a business and make a decent profit.

So, what level of insurance is adequate for your business? The truth is there is no straight answer other than it is most likely more than you are expecting.

While a business owner's general policy will fit most general needs, it may not cover everything. Let's look at the types of insurance policies available to pawn shop owners and whether or not you need any of them.

General Liability Insurance or Commercial Liability

What It Covers

It protects from a wide range of lawsuits that come from negligence while covering the cost of defense, claims for bodily harm or property damage, personal injury, and advertising damages related to libel or slander.

Required

Oftentimes this insurance is required for a physical business to be able to rent space or secure a loan.

Cost

Cost increases depending on exposure risk.

Product Liability Insurance

What It Covers

If your business makes, distributes, or sells a product then you are exposed to product liability since nearly all products have the potential to cause personal or property damage. This type of insurance will help protect your company from negligence, breach of warranty, product defects, and faulty instructions. It can also help cover you against the cost of recalls.

Required

While not required, it is often included in a business owner's policy. If you are providing parts or services to a larger company, you may be required to maintain this insurance as a part of your contract with them, so you do not become an added cost for them in case something goes awry.

Cost

The type of product you are manufacturing will determine the cost, as the risk factor is not the same for distributing a book as it is an electrical device.

Property Insurance

What It Covers

This insurance protects you against damage to your workspace. This can include any type of property damage events such as fires, floods, robberies, or leaks.

Required

This insurance is required if your business is going to occupy any type of physical space.

Cost

The cost can be affected by location and environmental risk factors.

Sprinkler Leakage Insurance

What It Covers

Sprinkler leakage is often included in property insurance, but you should ask if it is still available if you intend to take a closer look at it. This type of insurance is important for businesses that have important documents since recreating documents can be costly and sometimes impossible depending on the water damage on your computer equipment or your file cabinets.

Required

Typically not required, but rather suggested.

Cost

Premiums can increase depending on the cost to replace documents or equipment.

Professional Liability Insurance or 'Errors and Omissions' or Malpractice Insurance

What It Covers

Nearly all businesses providing services to the public should consider the risk that people may litigate for perceived or real damages. In order to not get too deep in a legal matter, it is suggested this is covered somewhere.

Required

Not typically a requirement, although some professional boards or associations will require it for members as an extra protection measure.

Cost

The price can vary greatly depending on your profession and the specific tort law in the state.

Umbrella Insurance

What It Covers

It is basically insurance that covers you beyond the dollar limits of a general policy.

Required

Not at all, but still relevant in its own way, depending on what it pertains to.

Cost

Often cheap since claims that reach the level of umbrella insurance are rare.

Worker's Compensation Insurance

What It Covers

This type of insurance provides compensation and medical care to employees injured on the job. The employee often gets compensation in exchange for giving up the right to sue the employer.

Required

If you have employees at your care, then the answer is a solid yes. Individual states have rules on workers' compensation, so you'll need to determine the level of coverage required in your state.

Cost

The cost will be influenced by the state laws and programs. It can also be influenced by the type of business you have and whether or not it is likely to have more claims. In addition, if your company has a history of making claims then your premiums will be higher.

Internet Business Insurance

What It Covers

This insurance is important for the small to medium-sized companies that do business online. It helps provide you with protection against security and privacy breaches. You may want to consider this policy even if you are a more offline business with multiple locations that digitally transmit information.

Required

No, as it is more of a factor that depends on what type of business you have and it is more on the low-risk than anything else.

Cost

This is a new type of insurance, and the cost often is determined by online activity and the type of information that needs to be protected, such as debit or credit cards, bank transactions, addresses, passwords, and other valuable customer and personal information.

Crime and Fidelity Insurance

What It Covers

This insurance helps protect you from workplace fraud and theft.

Required

Not typically, but may be required by a few business types.

Cost

You can reduce cost with strong policies and audit controls along with performing background checks on employees.

Business Interruption Expense Insurance

What It Covers

If your business should become disabled for any reason, this policy will cover financial outlays and reimburse any lost profits until the business can resume.

Required

No, but strongly recommended.

Cost

If you get this policy, you should make sure it has extra expense coverage. This can help you to rent an alternative location and resources while everything is getting sorted out in your original location.

Business Auto Insurance

What It Covers

If your employees spend a lot of time on the road in their own vehicles or company vehicles, then this insurance is very important.

Required

If your business owns or requires any kind of vehicle, this insurance is mandatory and is also known as fleet insurance.

Cost

The price of auto insurance varies by state.

Insurances are often seen as something only more paranoid individuals attain for matters that could be easily prevented with proper equipment.

For example, a water damage insurance is not necessary for a business located in a location where floods are improbable, and important files are placed in waterproof containers at a higher floor level, and online documents are constantly backed in USB drives or other methods.

However, if you have employees under your care, then it is imperative you get them insurance in order to give them a better work environment. These are preventative measures you must take regardless of what type of insurance you are considering.

Dealing with Merchandise

The demographics of those who will use pawnshop services cover a wide range of the public, communities, and households. Basically, the demographics of a pawnshop are anyone who needs to sell an item, buy an item, or need to get a loan. This can include wealthy people, businesspeople, the general public, students, and anyone in between.

Since a pawnshop will have multiple ways to make money, you'll need to attract more than one target market in order to be successful. If you are going to make money off short-term loans, then you'll need to attract customers who need cash immediately and don't want other sources of credit. However, a pawnshop also needs to attract those who want to purchase items by offering a good range of second-hand items for purchase.

Merchandising

When it comes to merchandising your pawnshop, there is a lot of items you'll be dealing with. We'll discuss a few of the more common items in detail in a moment, including what to look for and how to re-sell them. Before we start, I want to take a moment to simply discuss how you can stock your pawnshop with all this merchandise without having your store end up looking like a garage sale. Unlike retailers, you won't have control over what items you stock and how many of each you have; but there are some things you can do to keep your store in order and help keep the sales moving.

Follow the rules of sorting, arranging, cleaning, and repeating. For customers, the fun is in looking for a specific item and finding a great deal; but the customers don't want to dig through dusty bins full of random items. Sort and organize your merchandise into categories, so it is easier for customers to find. You should also create a schedule to keep things cleaned and maintained, so products are nice for the customers to see.

Second, it can help to add a little drama to your inventory. If possible, add attractive lighting and quality shelving. Not only does this make it easier for customers to shop, but it also makes things visually more appealing for your higher-end items.

Make sure you adjust merchandise daily. You'll likely move a wide range of products in and out of your store but try to view the store from the point of view of a new customer. If you tidy up your display and fill empty spaces on a daily basis, then you'll be able to keep the shop looking great and help attract customers.

When it comes to merchandise, keep the seasons in mind. Design displays with seasonal and holiday trends in mind in order to target the changing demands of customers. For example, around Christmas time, you can focus on tools, toys, and technology since these are popular gift items. On the other hand, around Valentine's Day jewelry displays can be a big draw.

Keep in mind the small stuff. To do this, place a rack by the register that has small and inexpensive items. This can help you generate some easy cash while also getting rid of the small items that may otherwise cause clutter in your store.

Make sure you always rotate your stock. Use your storage space to rotate merchandise, this will keep your customers engaged and prevent your shop from becoming cluttered with too much inventory. It is best to have a shop where customers can maneuver easily and find them rather than to have all your inventory on the shelves at the same time. If you find an item isn't selling, then you can put it in storage and bring it out later at a more appropriate time. If something does sell, then fill the empty space with something from your backstock. If someone is looking for something in particular and asks you for it, then you can go in back for it, and this can even help boost your customer service.

If there are items that are taking up too much space in your store or aren't selling well, then consider making a daily deal or advertise a special on occasion. This can also be a great way to increase customer interest.

Always try to attract your best customers. This is just a part of this goal. Determine which items offer you the biggest return and which customers are most likely to buy them. Then make these items either the bulk of your inventory or create displays that emphasize them.

Lastly, if needed, you can hire a professional merchandising expert. After the expert gets you started in the right direction, then you can use the learning experience to maintain your shop.

Having a well-stocked and laid out store can make all the difference. But it also matters what you bring into your store and how you attempt to sell it. So, let's consider some of the more common items and how you can buy and sell them. Of course, the first thing we need to consider is just where you'll get your merchandise from.

How to Source Merchandise

People can pawn anything valuable if they want cash. Most pawnshops won't check credit scores since there is already collateral for the loan. In order to source the best merchandise for your pawnshop, you need to understand not only what people are most likely to pawn, but also what is most likely in your state. Let's consider what some of the trends are in pawning to help you get a good idea of what to stock in your store.

Throughout the United States, the most popular category of pawned items is electronics. Among these, Apple products are the highest. However, there are some differences in regions. In the Southern and Western states, guns are often pawned at a higher rate. While in California and New York, luxury watches are the most pawned item. There are significant differences in what people pawn throughout the regions, but there are also differences in what men pawn versus women.

Nearly 30% of Americans throughout the United States pawn electronics. This is understandable since nearly everyone owns some type of valuable electronic, whether it is a personal computer, smartphone, gaming console, or television. The second-biggest category in the overall view of the United States is antiques. This is closely followed by tools, jewelry, and guns.

When it comes to the difference in individuals, it is a little simpler. Women are more likely to pawn apparel and jewelry, while men are more likely to pawn vehicles and guns. This shows that no matter where you are, there is likely to be a wide range of items that can come into your store. However, it is a good idea to pay attention to geography and regional patterns because this may tell you what is more likely to sell in your store. Consider the chart below to see what is most likely to be pawned and, as a result, purchased in your state. There are a few states not covered on the chart because they didn't have the necessary data.

State	Most Pawned Items
Alabama	Guns
Alaska	Guns
Arizona	Guns

Arkansas	Guns
California	Luxury Watches
Colorado	Vehicles
Delaware	Luxury Watches
Florida	Vehicles
Georgia	Guns
Hawaii	Jewelry
Idaho	Guns
Illinois	Electronics
Indiana	Antiques and Collectibles
Iowa	Precious Metals or Stones
Kansas	Guns
Kentucky	Guns
Louisiana	Luxury Watches

Maryland	Designer Clothes
Michigan	Vehicles
Minnesota	Precious Metals or Stones
Mississippi	Guns
Missouri	Antiques and Collectibles
Montana	Guns
Nebraska	Antiques and Collectibles
Nevada	Precious Metals or Stones
New Mexico	Precious Metals or Stones
New York	Luxury Watches
North Carolina	Guns
North Dakota	Jewelry
Ohio	Antiques and Collectibles
Oklahoma	Tools and Equipment

Oregon	Precious Metals or Stones
Pennsylvania	Antiques and Collectibles
South Carolina	Guns
South Dakota	Precious Metals or Stones
Tennessee	Guns
Texas	Designer Clothes
Utah	Guns
Virginia	Guns
Washington	Precious Metals or Stones
West Virginia	Guns
Wyoming	Precious Metals or Stones

Now that we know where to get merchandise and how to display it in your store let's look at some of the most common items and how you can deal with them.

Dealing with Gold and Silver

Recently, gold and silver prices are at a near-record level. This increases the buying and selling interest in gold and silver. At pawnshops, the most common form of gold and silver you'll deal with aside from jewelry is coins. Before buying or selling gold or silver coins, there are a few things you need to consider.

The first and foremost thing you need to do is have a bullion dealer that you know and trust. They should have both expertise and reputation.

Second, you should make sure you know the actual cost per ounce of the most common precious metals. Gold, silver, and platinum prices change daily, so check the daily prices before you make any transaction. You should expect to pay a higher price over the melt value for fractional gold pieces such as 1/10th, 1/4th, and ½ ounce than for one-ounce pieces.

You should also be aware of the fees and/or commissions that may be involved. For example, the average retail commission on a one-ounce American Eagle or Maple Leaf gold coin will be about five or six percent.

It is also a good idea to know about coins before you consider purchasing them or using them as collateral for loans. You can always research coins but knowing the most common ones can keep you informed and avoid your overpaying for coins.

Lastly, when it comes to gold and silver, as well as other precious metals, know that there are always risks involved. You may use these as collateral or purchases while prices are high, but when you go to sell, they may be lower. So be prepared. You may lose some money when working with precious metals.

Dealing with Guns

When it comes to owning a pawnshop, one thing you will certainly have to face dealing with is guns. Depending on the state where you own your business, it may actually be the bulk of your pawns. Whether or not you choose to deal with these items will be up to you, but if you are going to deal with guns, then you need to make sure you meet all the regulations and take all the proper precautions. Consider just a few of the ways that dealing with guns can present a legal issue if guidelines aren't followed:

Selling a firearm to an irresponsible party such as a mentally unstable, intoxicated, or other dangerous individual.

"Straw Sales" is a situation where a qualified buyer will purchase a firearm to give to or sell to a prohibited individual. There are ways to train your employees to avoid these types of sales. For example, when someone acts without knowledge of firearms, this should be a red flag.

Multiple and/or repeat sales to individuals. Under federal laws, this is anything over one firearm to the same individual in five days. Multiple sales or attempts need to be reported to the proper authorities.

Purchasing and selling of lost or stolen firearms. Often people may try to sell a firearm "off the books" and should be reported to the ATF.

If you still want to deal with guns, then there are some measures you can take to reduce risk, along with becoming legally licensed to sell firearms.

Have signs clearly posted on all entry doors notifying people that loaded firearms are prohibited in the store. You could also go a step further by asking that individuals pawning guns seek instructions from staff before bringing guns into the store. This not only gives customers a reminder but also provides the staff with a chance to prepare for the transaction.

As discussed earlier, another safety measure could be the hiring of a security guard who is posted at the door to check customers for firearms before they enter and ensuring they aren't loaded. This can be a good measure if you will be dealing with firearms regularly but may not be a viable option for those who only occasionally deal with firearms.

When instructing customers on how to proceed, ask for customers to bring weapons into the store in cases or containers. Ammunition should be brought in separately and never in the same container. If you sell ammunition, then it should be stored separately from firearms and away from customers.

You should also train your employees on how to properly accept firearms from those who are selling, trading, or pawning firearms. This training should include the safe handling of firearms and how to make sure all firearms are unloaded. All employees should assume firearms are loaded and use the proper procedures to clear a weapon each time it is handled. They must observe standard practices such as keeping the barrel pointed in a safe direction and using proper trigger discipline. Training could take the form of both classroom and range training.

Classroom training often includes the following:

- Statutory Requirements
- Use of deadly force
- Company policy on the use of force
- Firearms safety
- Safety practices
- Written exams

Range training often includes the following:

- Shooting stance
- Breathing control
- Trigger control

In addition to these basic safety precautions, it is also a legal requirement that you follow specific state and federal regulations. Transferring firearms ownership will require you to have a Federal Firearms License or FFL. This license may not be needed for non-firearm items like air guns, knives, ammunition, antique guns before 1899, and some gun parts, but this may vary by the state you are operating in.

There may also be restrictions on shipping. You need to properly ship firearms, and some carriers may not ship firearms. You can contact your local ATF field office if you have questions about shipping firearms.

Dealing with guns also comes with age restrictions that you need to follow. Only adults are able to enter into a contract. There may be age limits on other items depending on your state. You'll need to verify the seller's age by viewing their driver's license.

Typical age restrictions are the following:

- You generally need to be 18 to purchase firearms.

- You need to be at least 21 years old to buy pistol ammunition.
- You need to be at least 18 years old to buy rifle ammunition.
- You'll also be required to run a background check on anyone before selling a firearm.

It is best to know your state restrictions. For example, assault weapons can't be sold in California, while other states have limits on the type of ammunition that is legal. To learn about the specific laws in your state, you can visit the ATF website here:

https://www.atf.gov/firearms/state-laws-and-published-ordinances-firearms-33rd-edition

Dealing with Antiques and Collectibles

Another popular item you'll deal with as a pawnshop owner is antiques and collectibles. However, buying and selling antiques and collectibles is unlike any other item you'll work with. These items are often unique, and their values typically aren't influenced by economic trends and/or the stock market. This is a market that you need to approach carefully.

What to Know When Buying

When buying or pawning antiques, there are two things you need to take note of. First, you need to make a note of the condition of the item. Avoid any antiques that are in bad condition since they will sell for a lot less than items that are in pristine condition.

Second, you need to look for signs that an item is counterfeit. There are often cases of fraud in the market, so you need to make sure you aren't purchasing or using a clone as collateral. If people are trying to sell antiques for cash, then you especially want to be careful.

Before selling or accepting antiques or collectibles as loan collateral, you may need to determine how much an item is worth. There isn't really an easy answer to this question, and it will often require a little research on your park. Even with due diligence, you may find that getting the determined value from antique or collectible items may not happen.

The biggest value to an antique or collectible is in the negotiation between the buyer and seller. You need to set the price you're willing to pay for an item or the amount you're willing to put up for a loan. The customer may then try to get you to raise your price, but you should never go above what you feel you can reasonably get for an item.

How Professionals Value Antiques and Collectibles

Appraisers will value antiques and collectibles by looking at comparable values. This is done by finding a number of recorded sales for the same item you're researching in order to get a decently accurate value. You should always discard extremely high and low values and then average the remaining numbers. However, this can be difficult since you need to find an item that is in the same condition as the one you are looking to value. Often, you'll need to find similar items and adjust accordingly when valuing antiques and collectibles.

Where to Find Value Online

There are a number of resources you can find online when trying to determine the value of antiques or collectibles. Often there will be a website with guides, articles, or links to help you. You can also choose to use online appraisal services if you want to pay someone to give you an estimated value. Just remember that when you use an online price guide, you are often getting a single point in time when an item is sold rather than the current average selling price.

Another option is to go to an auction site and look up past results. This can give you a good way to compare multiple sales and get an approximate value. Just remember that online pricing can vary by site, and it may not reflect the negotiated price once an item sells at auction.

Doing Offline Research

You can also choose to use books at the local library to research the value of antiques and collectibles. If you often deal with specific antiques or collectibles, then you may want to consider purchasing a book or keeping a guide on hand to use when customers bring in an item to pawn. When using books, it is important to know that values are often higher than average, and you may not be able to get the same price as what is in the book.

Lastly, keep in mind that the value of items will vary depending on where you live. Some items will sell better in urban areas, while others do well in rural areas.

If you are looking to sell an antique or collectible in your shop, then you need to consider where and how you'll sell it. If you don't want to sell the item in your store, you can choose to sell it to an antiques dealer.

If you do this, you may get a wholesale price that is about one quarter to one half of what you could get selling it as a secondary market retailer. This is because the dealer is just like you, they have to consider overhead and may need to hold on to an item for a while in order to find the right buyer.

However, selling to a dealer means you may be able to move merchandise faster than selling it in your store.

You can also choose to sell your items online at auctions. This will often bring lower values as well. In order to get the most value for antiques and collectibles, you would do best by selling directly to the secondary market through your store.

The main advantage of online sales is that you can reach a larger potential buying audience. Determining the best way to sell your antiques and collectibles is often the final step in researching an item before selling it.

What to Know Before Selling

If you are looking to sell an antique or collectible in your pawnshop, then it is important to get as much value from an item as possible. In order to do this, there are two main things to keep in mind.

First, make sure you use the steps above to get the best value for your items. If you're in doubt, always get an item appraised.

Second, if you choose to sell to a dealer, then make sure they are reputed. Doing this will ensure you get the best return if someone doesn't repay their loan.

Dealing with Jewelry

Jewelry is similar to the items we've already discussed. Before using jewelry as collateral or purchasing it, you need to do your research. Look for good craftmanship and ensure the jewelry is authentic. Ask lots of questions, and if something seems off, then question the authenticity or ownership of the piece. For really expensive jewelry, you should ask for receipts or certificates of authenticity. Even if a piece isn't valued too high for resale, consider the value of melting the jewelry down. This would be similar to considering the gold and silver value.

Once you need to resell jewelry, it is important to give careful consideration to how you sell it. Often jewelry is the biggest moneymaker for pawnshops outside of the loans. This means you should take extra time and effort when it comes to displaying your jewelry effectively. Stocking your inventory is only a part of the issue. The other is to display it in a way that will attract customers. To do this, you can use the following tips.

First, is to carefully consider the lighting. This is both in your display cases as well as interior lights in general. LED lighting is best since it will highlight and accentuate the diamonds in jewelry. This lighting may be more expensive but think of the returns you'll get in both sales and lighting durability. Also, make sure the ambient lighting around jewelry cases is bright and directed right in order to reduce glare.

Second, as with most inventory, make sure you rotate it based on the season. Have a bold red backdrop during Valentine's day while using softer backgrounds around Mother's Day. In summer, add fresh flowers. Whenever you change the look of your display case, it will attract attention.

Be sure to highlight the precious stones. Larger diamond pieces need to be displayed in a distinct and unique manner. Separate them from the rest of the inventory with a special arrangement. Spotlight the pieces by providing a description of the color, clarity, and size. You may even want to consider displaying a GIA certification.

If needed, you can also choose to use props. Often the smallest difference can help your potential customers connect with a piece and encourage them to buy. For example, place an antique broach on top of an old book to help highlight the era.

Lastly, consider grouping your items by category. Perhaps keep earrings separate from bracelets. This will often make it easier for customers to find things and reduce confusion for them.

Creating the best jewelry display will take some time and consideration. However, the work in selling jewelry doesn't stop here. Just because you may be able to entice your customers to look doesn't mean they'll turn into a purchase. This is where you need to use emotion in five tips to help you sell jewelry.

First, make sure you get the customer talking about who they are buying the jewelry for. People love talking about hobbies and interests. When you do this, it can help you identify their taste and know what people are likely to want. It also helps the people to think about why they are buying the jewelry so they may be open to spending more.

Second, make the customer feel important by asking for their opinion. When you make people more comfortable while purchasing jewelry, they'll feel more important, which can help you turn it into a sale.

The best way to sell emotion is to focus on the occasion, or the reason for the purchase. Talk about how special the Christmas season is and how the perfect gift can make a person feel. This is helpful when you have already discussed a persons' interests since you can further direct them towards a good reason to purchase a piece of jewelry.

Ensure your customers feel unique by using terms that promote rarity. The jewelry is hand-selected with the person in mind. The jewelry is unique, and they won't find it anywhere else. Everyone wants to feel special, and if they do, they are more likely to buy from you.

Lastly, remember people love a good story. So, it pays to be a good storyteller. People are often buying the story and not the item. Have a story being each piece of jewelry, and you'll increase your chances of making a sale.

Now that we have discussed getting inventory to your store, we should look at another valuable aspect of your store, the employee. The items you bring in and sell at your store are only as good as your employees. You need to hire and train them so you can be comfortable leaving them in charge of making appropriate deals while you aren't there.

Staffing a Pawnshop

Hiring, training, and retaining employees for a pawnshop can be a bit of a challenge. There is more to it than simply choosing the right employee; you also need to know how to train and retain them so they can gain confidence in the work environment of a pawnshop. Let's look at what you can do to have success in each of these areas.

Hiring

Hiring employees is all about attitude. When someone shows up at your shop for an interview, give them a few moments on the sales floor. Observe how they interact with other employees and customers. Are they making the most of their time or simply trying to stay out of the way? First impressions are key in the hiring process, and you'll want to hire a confident person with a good personality.

When you move to the interview process, you'll want to pay attention to the following:

- Appearance - Is the individual well-groomed and dressed for the occasion?

- Are they taking notes, and do they ask questions?

- What is their body language saying - are they confident?

- Do you feel they are being truthful in their answers?

How do they speak about their former employers? It is okay for them to speak their mind, but they should do it tactfully, and they shouldn't degrade previous employers.

Be open and honest with potential employees during the interview process. Let them know what really goes into working with you and be sure to give them both the positives and negatives.

At the end of the interview, do they ask questions? It is a positive sign if they ask you what the next step is and when they will be likely to hear a response from you.

If possible, have another brief interview done with another manager or employee. It is always best to have a minimum of two opinions. It is always a good idea to have one interview be with someone they will work with regularly or a supervisor to ensure they connect well.

If the interview goes well, then schedule a shadow session, best during a busy time of the day so you can see how they do, and they can see how the business works. This can give everyone a good idea of how much they can handle. During these sessions, watch how they interact with other employees and clients. You want to hire an ambitious person as well as a strong personality. You want to hire for the long term in this business and not the short term.

Once you've chosen the best employees for the job, there is still more work to do. Now you need to focus on providing them the training they need to successfully do the job and be comfortable working in the pawnshop business.

Training

Quite a few employers simply throw new employees into the work and don't focus on what they need. Don't be one of these employers, and rather think about how you learned the ropes. Think about what your employees want to learn and treat them as an investment to your business. Keep the following in mind when training your new employees.

Keep new employees away from the sales floor for at least the first two to three days. Take them somewhere where they can learn the business and the specifics of your business. Make sure they are aware of what you expect from them when it comes to customer service, daily tasks, and team goals. Once they are done, then you can move them to the sales floor.

For the next few days, pair the new employee with an appropriately experienced employee. Make sure you compensate employees for helping train new hires since they may earn fewer commissions during this time since they'll be away from customers. Ensure the individual you choose to train is experienced and reliable.

Either you or a manager should spend time with the new hire each day before they finish their shift. Answer any questions they have and go through their day. Make sure new hires always leave on a positive note no matter how difficult the day was. The first week is often the most crucial and will often make the difference between a long-term employee and a quick exit.

The following week review the first week. Discuss the good and the bad while restating what you expect from them in the future. If needed, quiz them in order to ensure they are retaining the information you want them to. Perhaps have them go through a few transactions or look up inventory to ensure they are confident with the computer system.

Once the training is complete, you will have a strong employee who is in it for the long haul. However, you need to be in it as well. You need to be focused on retaining the employee.

Retention

One of the biggest issues facing employers today is the retention of motivated employees. To do this, you need to make your shop an attractive place to work. This doesn't always mean good pay and benefits, but there are other things to consider, such as appreciation, challenge, growth, and opportunities. Consider some examples of what you can do to retain excellent employees.

Treat your employees with respect. Treat them how you want to be treated. Then they'll appreciate coming to work for you and will be less likely to look elsewhere.

Have a clear set of rules and then ensure they are applied fairly. Have a written set of policies that apply to all employees, no matter what their age or seniority.

Have clear communication with all employees. Have a set schedule for staff meetings, ideally weekly, so that employees can be kept up to date on anything new.

Make sure you listen to your employees. Keep yourself available for feedback, both good and bad.

Be flexible and know that your employees have personal lives that can change suddenly. If you are flexible with your scheduling, then you'll be an attractive place for people to work.

Reward excellent performance and remember it doesn't always have to be about the money. Bonuses and pay raises are always appreciated by employees, but you can also offer other forms of recognition and acclaim.

Ensure the work environment is fun. Hold store events and keep the good energy flowing.

Lastly, recognize employees' abilities and look for ways to increase and use their potential. Perhaps pay for educational opportunities such as GIA classes. This return on investment will pay off well.

Doing these things will help you get the best employees and have a great working environment. But you also need to focus on getting customers to help maintain your business. To do this, you need to have a strong promotion, advertising, and marketing campaign. Let's consider these next.

Promotion, Advertising, and Marketing

Many people typically have a negative view of pawnshops. They view them as a place where people go to pawn items when they are down on their luck and need quick money. Pawnshops are starting to gain more mainstream popularity, but it still pays to have a good promotional, advertising, and marketing campaign to help draw people to your pawnshop for pawning as well as buying. Let's look at some things that can help you in these areas.

Image Management

The first thing you need to do is improve the perceptions people have of your pawnshop. This means you need an attractive entrance to encourage people to come in and see what you have to offer. If you only have windows crammed with displays, then they are likely to pass you by. Then once they enter, be sure to have a clean and well-organized store.

Encourage people to check out your place by holding a grand opening and advertising on local media. Invite people to bring things for expert appraisers. Have items on hand and experts to answer questions. This can help provide a good image for your business and keep it in mind for when people are in need of your services.

Since most pawnshops are found in low-income neighborhoods, it can be a good idea to help revitalize the area. Consider installing things like benches or plants to make the area more attractive. Have good lighting and secure parking, so customers feel comfortable coming to your store.

Perhaps the most important part if running your business is in the advertising. There are a few things you can do to improve the advertising of your business. Let's look at some top ideas to help you get started:

Make sure your advertisements and promotions highlight any specialty areas you feature.

Help customers by offering links to item histories, manufacturers, or production methods when offering items for sale online.

Consider offering coupons and incentives to draw customers into your store.

Feature visits from appraisers and/or experts so people can come in and view what you have to offer while getting items appraised without the pressure to sell.

Perhaps you can offer classes to help people increase their knowledge on things like coin collecting.

Starting a newsletter is a great way to keep your customers in the know and increase the chance of repeat business. There are plenty of free services that allow you to send out email newsletters each month. A newsletter doesn't need to be complex; it can be as simple as a few photos of new items and some interesting trivia. Collect email addresses from clients at checkout if they are interested.

Make sure your website is SEO optimized. Search engine optimization is often free and can increase the visibility of your website. Getting your website ranked higher in the search engines will ensure people locate your business before others.

Consider Facebook ads, an easy and affordable option for advertising. Facebook ads allow you to geo-target customers and tailor your ads to their interests and demographics. This means you can advertise to a specific location, age group, and gender.

You can also practice good public relations in your local community. Consider ads in the local newspaper and other local avenues of advertising.

Have a loyalty system in place for repeat customers. Give them a card that you stamp whenever they purchase something and then offer some form of a discount once they reach a specific number of purchases.

Once you get people into your store, you need to keep them there by making it a good experience. This is where customer relations and good customer service are key. So, let's look at these areas next.

Customer Relations and Customer Service

The first step in customer relations and customer service is to identify your most valuable customers. To do this, you need to always be improving your customer experience. Without customers, a pawnshop would have no business. So, you want to keep customers happy and returning to your store. In addition to advertising, you need to make sure you put your marketing efforts into the right area. Studies have shown that if you provide customers with better service, then profits increase. This means you need to focus on your customers if you want to grow your business. However, this doesn't mean you should treat all customers the same, and you should focus most of your efforts on customers who offer long term value for your shop. To identify these customers, you need to evaluate the following areas.

First, consider the sales minus the cost. Many companies choose to rank customers based on how many sales they do. However, this doesn't take into account the most important part of the equation. While customers can do a lot of business, you need to consider the overall cost of making sales. All customers provide some level of revenue, but sometimes the cost to fulfill a sale could exceed the value you get from multiple sales.

Not all revenue is the same, and timing is important. For example, if you sell electronics in your shop, it will likely make its most revenue in the fourth quarter during holiday shopping, but not as much during the first quarter. A sale in the off-peak seasons is going to be more profitable because it fills an unused production capacity or sometimes can be sold at a higher price.

You should also focus on customers that offer referrals and word of mouth marketing for your business. In an age that is focused on the internet, consumers turn to social media for reviews, posts, and tweets for information more than commercial advertising. If a customer is willing to advertise for your company and spread their experience, then this can be a strong endorsement for your business.

Customer retention is also important. It is less costly for your business to retain customers than it is to find new ones. Most businesses focus the majority of their marketing budget and efforts on attracting new customers and don't focus on the customers who are leaving. If a company has been with your business for a long time, they will often be more profitable, may buy more products, and will often become a walking billboard for your business.

Consider offering add-on products and services. Customers who buy more than one product are more profitable because acquiring the customer is done with a larger sales base. This is done through efficient customer service.

A valuable thing for small businesses such as the one you're starting is the customer's brand. If customers do business with a well-known brand, then they can build a reputation. If someone well known buys a product from you and then talks about it, your sales are going to increase. This can happen even with a regular customer at a small business, just make sure people talk about their experience with you.

Lastly, make it easy to share feedback on social media. Most people never provide feedback on business or their products. Often the only reviews come from those who are extremely satisfied or extremely dissatisfied. However, all opinions and feedback are valuable, so be sure to ask for them.

Once you've identified your top customers, you also want to successfully work with them. The bulk of a pawnshop business is on loans with items as collateral. Therefore, you need to have the important skill of qualifying your customers. This is similar to vetting new employees and seeing if they will be a good fit for your shop.

Everyone in the pawnshop industry has had a time when a customer has gone through a half-hour process only to walk away from the deal. No matter the reason, it is important for you to qualify customers to bring in business and increase a satisfied client base. Let's look at how you can do this.

The process starts with the sales counter the moment the client arrives. Make sure you see and acknowledge the client as they come in the front door. Keep an eye on the customer body language as they walk up to the counter and observe how they handle their items. This gives you a good indication of how to proceed with the transaction. Always trust your instincts since they're often not wrong. From here, it is all about asking the right questions. The following are the right questions to ask and what you can learn from them.

Ask if they want to make a loan but avoid using the word pawn. A lot of people won't realize that what they are actually doing is making a loan with your store. When people hear the term pawn, they are thinking of selling an item. If the person isn't interested in a loan, then you need to ask a follow-up question.

Ask if they want to sell the item and look at their reaction. Do they show emotional attachment, do they hesitate when answering; these are valuable cues. If they want to sell, then buy it at a fair price. Asking this at the start will save you a lot of time and effort later in the process.

Once you know whether the customer is looking for a loan or a sale, then you need to ask how much they need. This is where you'll start talking about money. If they ask for a very high or low amount, then you need to proceed with caution. While they may be testing you to see how far you'll go, some people are trying to get rid of an item that may not be legal. Most people will come to you with an idea of what an item is worth and will ask for a reasonable amount.

Keep the customer talking and ask them to tell you more about the item. See if they have an emotional attachment, if they need it for something essential or if it belongs to someone they know. Dig as much as you can but be gentle. If someone is attached to an item, they are more likely to return with the loan amount and pick up the item.

Always rely on your tools as needed. Dig digger by looking up their customer history if they've been to your store before. Do they often return to pick up items or only high-end items? This will help you to determine if taking the time to process a loan is worth it or if it will be easier to simply buy the item.

If the answer is to process a loan, then ask the customer how long they need the money. Be suspicious of answers that aren't normal. If the customer has a specific time in mind, then they have likely thought about things and are more likely to return for the item. If they mention local laws or give you an "about" time, then they may still be telling the truth, but you will want to be a little more careful. The answer here is going to tell you where the transaction is headed.

Help your customers and judge their potential by offering text reminders. The text reminders can tell them when to make a payment. When you use this as a part of your process, then you'll be more likely to have someone sign up for text messages rather than simply asking them if they want to receive text messages. While you won't know until you send a text message, if it doesn't bounce back to you, then you'll know the individual wants their item back. If someone changes their number and/or doesn't pick up an item, then put a note in the computer in case they return in the future.

Lastly, ask if they have any questions about the contract. Make sure they understand the contract and offer to go over it with them again if needed. If the customer asks questions here, then it is a good sign they'll pick up their item. If a customer doesn't seem interested in what will happen, then there is a good chance the item will end up in your inventory.

Asking the right questions and qualifying customers can often make the process of offering a loan a lot easier. It will also increase customer satisfaction, so you are more likely to get return business.

These little things will help your business stand out for people to come back and refer new people to you. However, this isn't to say you will never have a dissatisfied customer. If this does happen, you also need to focus on how you handle it.

Every angle of customer service is important, even if you are connecting with an unhappy customer. You may not have a customer return, but at least leaving them with a good impression means they won't talk about your shop negatively to others.

No matter what the issues are, use the key points below when dealing with customers who aren't satisfied:

- Remember that it is always about the customer.

- View it as an opportunity to help your customer and allow your business to improve.

- Listen attentively to what the customer has to say and take appropriate notes.

- Acknowledge the customer's issue and make it clear that you are there to help them.

- It is critical that you address issues punctually and take accountability.

- Make sure you call them back as soon as possible.

- Try to resolve the issue as soon as possible.

- Avoid a long email discussion, do things by phone.

- Take point in the process, and don't take the blame if the issue isn't related to your company.

- Document the situation and how it was resolved so those who have to deal with the customer later will know how to handle it or will know the situation has been resolved.

Inventory and POS Systems

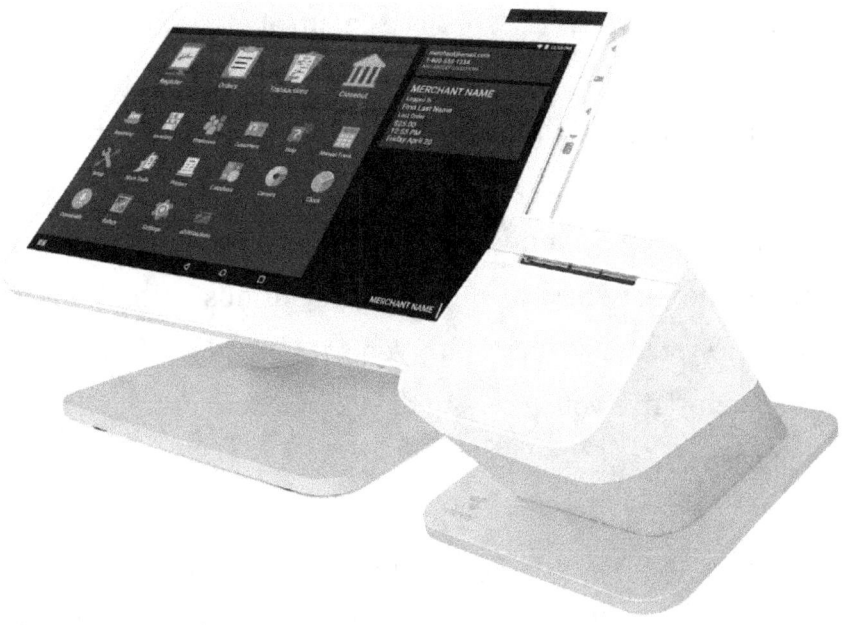

Nearly all types of businesses require some type of software. In pawnshops, this will also help you to be more successful. When we are talking about business software, we aren't suggesting something like Word or Excel; rather, software is something that helps you run all the vital elements of your business, control costs, and automate as many functions as possible. Even small businesses like your pawnshop could benefit from an accounting program that helps you keep your books, send invoices, make payroll, and help you pay taxes. However, there are also some more advanced software options for pawnshops that can help you run the critical parts of your business.

Larger businesses will use advanced software in order to manage sales leads, track projects, control manufacturing, and other vital functions. Large businesses understand the investment and why it is important to choose the right business software and work to keep it going. Software companies provide support and can help provide you with an understanding of how it will improve your business. Using a software system not only helps you get tasks done faster, but it also helps give you access to the experiences of the larger businesses.

However, a software system should be viewed as an investment. The money you put into a software system needs to provide you with a good return. A large company may spend hundreds of thousands and even into the millions for a software program, but as a new startup, you won't have this much of a budget. When you consider the cost of software, you need to consider not only the cost of the new software but also the annual maintenance of your system.

As a small business, you can use advanced software to help you successfully run your business. Nearly all small businesses use some kind of accounting software. However, this is a simple tool, and you should try to find one of the lowest cost options you can. Once you find one, you should learn all you can learn about all the options and how the software can help you save and make more money.

Before you purchase any kind of business software, you need to research the company behind your options. Once you have done this, you want to learn about what the software can do for you and what the pros and cons are to each system. Take the time to talk to the sales representatives so you get a feel for the company you'll be working with. Are the representatives just trying to sell you the software, or are they asking questions about your business and helping guide you in the right direction?

Does the representative understand your business environment and offer a solution to help you through the use of their software? Remember that a business software system is more than a piece of software, it should be viewed as a business solution. Don't make the choice easily since it will cost you a lot of money in the long run, learning how to operate and keep it up to date. Software is a valuable investment for your pawnshop business. Once you are up and running, you'll need to start focusing on ways to grow your pawnshop.

How to Grow Your Pawnshop

Once you have your pawnshop up and running, you'll want to start thinking about how you can grow and make your business even more successful. There are many ways to do this, and most of them center around the successful day to day operations of your business.

I've talked with many of the top business owners in this industry to get their idea on the best business practices to help grow your pawnshop. The following are the tips I've learned.

Displaying Electronics

If you market in electronics and TVs in particular, then there are two things that will help your TVs sell: picture and price. TVs that aren't turned on won't generate a lot of interest. Even an older TV with a great picture and an affordable price will sell better when it is turned on to showcase it. You can even enhance the view by attaching a Blu-Ray player.

Firearms Tips

When it comes to dealing with firearms, there are several ideas to help. First, when it comes to stocking guns, most long guns such as shotguns and rifles will be stored behind the counter at least six feet from customers. Even handguns will be under glass in a case that may be obscured by scratches and/or glare. Therefore, make sure all the sales tags have the following details in large print: Manufacturer, Model, Caliber, and Price. Most people purchasing guns will know the gun on sight, but the average customer may need some guidance. Save everyone time and frustration with these sales tags so the process can be simple and smooth.

Second, you may want to consider carrying new firearms in your inventory. While the margins aren't as good as some other categories, it can help increase new customer traffic and increase your income. The focus is to get customers to buy at your store and make it a habit. Even if you only make

20% on a sale rather than 40%, it will still be better than no sale because you don't have an inventory that can compete with the competition. You'll also be able to determine if there are additional needs from your customers.

Lastly, you may want to consider selling add-ons if you are selling firearms. You can make additional money by offering additions such as holsters, ammunition, and cleaning kits. These often will typically see great margins and can offset the higher margin that comes with selling newer firearms.

Involve the Community

This is perhaps one of the best things you can do as the owner of a pawnshop. Reach out to a community organization that can help you generate good customers. Talk to them about organizing a community event such as a BBQ in the summer. You can supply the goods and the organization can keep all the profits. Set up the event in your parking lot or store. This can be a great way to gain new customers while also giving back to the community.

Advertise these events through a variety of means, including Facebook and flyers, to generate as much attention as possible. You may even want to consider doing a raffle to increase interest in your business and generate even more money for the organization you're supporting. Plus, it can be a great way to get rid of inventory that isn't moving. Imagine the word of mouth marketing that will come from this and how many new customers it may generate for your shop.

Use Your Managers

If you are growing, you'll start adding employees. Soon you'll turn over some work to managers, and when you do, it is important to use them and let them do their job. Managers are often the highest-paid employees in a store, and you need to trust them with all daily operational decisions. Make sure they know when they need to consult you as the owner - such as when there is an unusual transaction or if the value of a transaction goes over a specific limit. Aside from this, try to avoid micromanaging. If you do need to offer feedback, make sure you do it in private, so you don't undermine the manager's authority in front of other employees.

In addition, you want to give your managers a proper area from which to manage. This is known as the manager's circle and is typically somewhere in front of the counter. This allows them to greet customers as they enter the store and can gauge their intent as they approach. The manager needs to be the facilitator for transactions, entertain customers, and set up a selling relationship between the shop and the customer.

In the same way, it is also important that you have your manager be the one to answer the phone. A pawnshop may receive about 50 to 150 calls a day. These calls can vary, but a lot will involve questions or issues about your business. In this case, who do you want to be the one talking to your customers? The manager is the one who has the best chance to help existing customers or persuade new ones. Consider having a cordless or hands-free phone system that your manager can always keep on them.

Take Care of Your Employees

Just as with your managers, you want to focus on and take care of your employees. One way you can encourage your employees to boost business is by setting sales goals and offering pay bonuses. Set a personal, attainable sales goal for each employee at the start of the month. For each goal, they achieve they receive a bonus. This gets employees excited, increases revenue for your store, and rewards employees who work extra hard.

Make sure you also recognize the employees for their accomplishments. Have an email that goes out to your employees that provides virtual applause for employees that offer great customer service or go above and beyond, such as those with big sales or large loans. This will help to encourage the behavior you want among employees. Recognizing your employees is important.

Maintain Your Store

It may seem obvious, but make sure you are keeping both your sales floor and the outside area of your store clean. This means more than just keeping things tidy. When your store is clean, organized, and has proper lighting, it will show professionalism and give your customers a sense of honesty and trust. This can turn into larger loans since customers will feel safer leaving items in your care. It will also make it easier when you need to hire new employees and retain existing ones since they will appreciate where they work.

Improve Your Loan Game

There are several things you can do to improve your approach to the loans, how you handle them, and how you can encourage people to repay them.

First, if your software features it, take a picture of a loan. It often doesn't cost much to have a camera attached to a terminal, and it can be a valuable investment. With this, you can document the condition of an item during the transaction. It also helps to discourage theft and fake loans.

Once an item is in your shop, you can also set up text reminders for pawned items and layaways. Nearly 90 percent of people have cell phones, and communication through text is becoming increasingly popular; this is great for those who own a pawnshop business. Customers are more appreciative of a text reminder than a collection call. Set your software to send a text reminder to those with loans at least ten days before the due date. With the text message, you can improve your redemption, renewal, and extension rates.

Improving Your Jewelry Game

There are multiple ways to improve your jewelry game, but there are three main things I want to cover. Some of them I've already discussed, but it is a good reminder.

First, make sure all higher value jewelry is uniquely displayed. Jewelry shoppers experience a common condition known as "eye fatigue," a condition wherein less than 30 seconds of shopping the jewelry all starts to blend together. Most trays for jewelry will hold between 16 to 64 rings, while bracelets can be 6 to 25 per tray. So how do you make your higher value stand out from the rest? Consider creating a separate display for higher value items with clearly marked tags that are easy to read. Combine this with proper lighting and higher-end jewelry will sell much easier and faster.

This brings us to the second tip, which is to improve the LED lighting in your jewelry cases. Jewelry is often the largest component of a loan balance within the inventory, and you need to focus on it. With just a few more dollars to change the lighting, you can dramatically increase the sales of one of your biggest assets. Lighting will enhance diamonds and brighten all jewelry displays. LED lights will also last longer to reduce overhead costs.

Lastly, consider cleaning a customer's jewelry for free. This will easily get a conversation started, especially for those who are in the market for jewelry. It doesn't cost you much to clean the jewelry and opens a discussion so you can gauge what they may be interested in purchasing. It practically guarantees a satisfied customer, even if they don't purchase anything. You can also add them to a want list, so when a jewelry item they want arrives, you can call them and get a sale.

Improved Inventory Management

When it comes to your inventory, there are several things you need to do to keep your shop in top shape and help it to grow. Let's look at several of these to see how this important part of your business can help you to stay successful and grow.

First, make sure you do a monthly audit of your safe and firearms. Theft is an all too common reality in the pawnshop business. You deal with a lot of cash, jewelry, and firearms, so there are plenty of theft opportunities. You should have a monthly, yet random, schedule to check jewelry loans/layaways and ensure all your firearms are accounted for with correct serial numbers. This good track record is also very important for the ATF.

You may even want to take this as far as doing a daily gun and jewelry count. While this may be obvious to some, you also need to make sure you are doing it right. Do you have the same employee or manager doing the counting each day? Are you verifying the counts independently? Are you rotating the duty to other people? It can be a good idea to have two people check the count separately and then have then sign twice a day for both opening and closing to help deter thefts.

Another thing you want to do on a daily basis is to walk your pulls and drops. This is a less obvious way that thefts can happen, but when things get pulled from pawn to inventory, it is a good way to lose merchandise. Often a manager may provide an employee with a list of pawns and just assume they are successfully moved to the sales floor. But you need to make sure of this? You can easily print a list of pulls at the end of the day and double-check that they are all on the sales floor and not leaving with the employee. Keep this list on hand in a binder so you can easily track inventory or, better yet, keep an electronic record in your software.

All pawnshops have to deal with aged inventory at some point. At the end of the day, consider printing out a report that shows you all your inventory turning 90 days old. Find the item on your sales floor and either move it to a new position, rotate it off the sales floor, or re-price it. Keep this list as well, so you can track what inventory is selling and what is staying. If something stays longer than 90 days, it can be a good idea to stop stocking that item in your inventory.

Another way to deal with aging inventory is to consider online sales options. For many pawnshop owners, the biggest issue is inventory that doesn't sell. Consider that today most people have a cell phone and do their shopping online. If you need to pull an item because it hasn't sold in 90 days or more, then consider taking a quick picture of it and posting it online. If you have a software program with an e-commerce solution, use it to help sell your aging inventory online. There are plenty of options, and you'll reach a larger audience that may even pay you more for it than you would get in your store.

Use Facebook

It cannot be stressed enough how important it is to use social media when marketing and advertising your business. Be sure to create a business page on Facebook for your shop. Use incentives within your store to generate "followers" on Facebook. You can also post aging inventory on the Facebook Marketplace. From there, you can use the "boost" feature to promote both higher value items and/or special store events and sales. Facebook gives you a great chance to profile users and generate qualified customers for your business. There is a lot of great things you can do with this social media outlet, and most of it won't cost you a lot.

Improve Sales

There are two great things you can be doing to increase sales that I guarantee you haven't thought about because I didn't until someone told me about them. Let's consider two great ways to improve sales in your shop.

The first thing you want to do is encourage your employees to offer layaway sales. Most people make impulse purchases when at a pawnshop. In order to improve your chance of a sale, you should offer both a sales price and a "minimum down" to enter a layaway option. Managers should be taught to monitor conversations between employees and potential customers to ensure that the option of layaway is communicated. The best part of offering layaways is that a customer often needs to make multiple visits to pay off their layaway, and this gives you greater chances to interact with them to improve customer satisfaction.

Another great thing you should do is consider adding want lists. If a customer comes in looking for something specific, add their name and number to a want list. Then if an item comes in for sale, you know you have a guaranteed buyer. You can often even program your software to alert you when there is a match. You can even use this as a reward system for your employees. And it offers you a great way to increase customer satisfaction which means better word of mouth advertising.

Use Your Software

We've already discussed the benefits of software, and it is best to remind you to use it. Utilize your software to get its full value. Know what the demographics are of your customers, evaluate your employee performance, discover what inventory sells; basically, the more you can learn about your business through the software, then the better your decision making, which can make your business more successful and increase growth. If you need help, call the technical support to teach you all that your software can offer your business.

Learn from the Competition

Lastly, always keep an eye on what competitors are doing. Know how much they loan on typical items since you can be sure your customers are aware. Then do your best to match what they are offering. If you can't compete with them on a financial level, then consider other ways to offer something the competition doesn't have. If you find business is slowing, then there is likely a reason, and it typically has to do with your competitors.

When you do these things, you can see your business become successful, and the more success you have, the easier it will be to grow your business. As your business grows you can repeat these steps to continue the success. Then you can take advantage of the growth expected in this industry.

Conclusion

Pawnbrokers and pawnshops provide a unique form of credit for the individual in need of cash. They also provide a number of other retail business solutions. As the economic gap continues to widen, the demand for the services of a pawnshop will continue to grow. Banks are not an easy option for those who need to get cash to pay off debts or pay for costly services. Also, pawnshop loans don't affect credit scores like bank loans.

With the growth potential of this industry, it is a great self-employment option to get started today. After reading this, hopefully, you have a good idea of how to start, run, and grow a pawnshop business. So, you can go out and get started today before the market gets saturated. Become a pawnbroker today and see how you can help people while having a great small business.

I hope this book has inspired and informed you. If it has helped you in any way, would you please consider leaving a review at the site where you purchased this book? Reviews help my efforts reach more people, and I also value your feedback. Thank you in advance.

Appendix: State by State Requirements

Alabama

Type of License: Alabama Pawnbroker License

Issuing Authority: Alabama State Banking Department's Bureau of Loans

Filing Fees: $150

Other Requirements: Annual Renewal

Notes: An application, extensive supporting documentation, and the filing fee are required.

Alaska

Type of License: Alaska Pawnbroker License

Issuing Authority: Alaska Division of Corporations, Business and Professional Licensing

Filing Fees: $1,000

Other Requirements: Biennial Renewal

Notes: An application, extensive supporting documentation, and the filing fee are required.

Arkansas

A state pawnbroker license is not required in the State of Arkansas. However, in order to operate as a pawnbroker, you may be required to get licensed on the local level, as well as you may be required to meet other state requirements. Talk to your local authorities to see what is required before opening your pawnshop.

Arizona

A state pawnbroker license is not required in the State of Arizona. However, in order to operate as a pawnbroker, you may be required to get licensed on the local level, as well as you may be required to meet other state requirements. Talk to your local authorities to see what is required before opening your pawnshop.

California

Type of License: California Pawnbroker License

Issuing Authority: The California municipality or county where your business will be operating.

Filing Fees: $300

Other Requirements: Biennial Renewal

Notes: An application, extensive supporting documentation, and the filing fee are required.

Colorado

A State pawnbroker license is not required in the State of Colorado. However, in order to operate as a pawnbroker, you may be required to get licensed on the local level, as well as you may be required to meet other state requirements. Talk to your local authorities to see what is required before opening your pawnshop.

Connecticut

Type of License: Connecticut Pawnbroker License

Issuing Authority: Connecticut Division of State Police

Filing Fees: $50

Other Requirements: Annual Renewal

Notes: An application, extensive supporting documentation, and the filing fee are required.

District of Columbia

Type of License: District of Columbia Pawnbroker License

Issuing Authority: DC Department of Consumer and Regulatory Affairs

Filing Fees: $1,500

Other Requirements: Biennial Renewal

Notes: An application, extensive supporting documentation, and the filing fee are required.

Delaware

Type of License: Delaware Pawnbroker License

Issuing Authority: Delaware State Police

Filing Fees: $50

Other Requirements: Annual Renewal

Notes: An application, extensive supporting documentation, and the filing fee are required.

Florida

Type of License: Florida Pawnbroker License

Issuing Authority: Florida Department of Agriculture and Consumer Services

Filing Fees: $300

Other Requirements: Annual Renewal

Notes: An application, extensive supporting documentation, and the filing fee are required.

Georgia

A state pawnbroker license is not required in the State of Georgia. However, in order to operate as a pawnbroker, you may be required to get licensed on the local level, as well as you may be required to meet other state requirements. Talk to your local authorities to see what is required before opening your pawnshop.

Hawaii

A state pawnbroker license is not required in the State of Hawaii. However, in order to operate as a pawnbroker, you may be required to get licensed on the local level, as well as you may be required to meet other state requirements. Talk

to your local authorities to see what is required before opening your pawnshop.

Iowa

A state pawnbroker license is not required in the State of Iowa. However, in order to operate as a pawnbroker, you may be required to get licensed on the local level, as well as you may be required to meet other state requirements. Talk to your local authorities to see what is required before opening your pawnshop.

Idaho

A state pawnbroker license is not required in the State of Idaho. However, in order to operate as a pawnbroker, you may be required to get licensed on the local level, as well as you may be required to meet other state requirements. Talk to your local authorities to see what is required before opening your pawnshop.

Illinois

Type of License: Illinois Pawnbroker License

Issuing Authority: Illinois Department of Financial and Professional Regulation's Division of Banking

Filing Fees: $765

Other Requirements: Annual Renewal

Notes: An application, extensive support documentation, and the filing fee are required.

Indiana

Type of License: Indiana Pawnbroker License

Issuing Authority: Indiana Department of Financial Institutions

Filing Fees: $1,000

Other Requirements: Annual Renewal

Notes: An application, extensive support documentation, and the filing fee are required.

Kansas

Type of License: Kansas Pawnbroker License

Issuing Authority: Kansas Attorney General's Office

Filing Fees: $25

Other Requirements: Annual Renewal

Notes: An application, extensive support documentation, and the filing fee are required.

Kentucky

A state pawnbroker license is not required in the State of Kentucky. However, in order to operate as a pawnbroker, you may be required to get licensed on the local level, as well as you may be required to meet other state requirements. Talk to your local authorities to see what is required before opening your pawnshop.

Louisiana

Type of License: Pawnbroker License

Issuing Authority: Office of Financial Institutions

Filing Fees: $100

Other Requirements: Annual Renewal

Notes: An application, extensive support documentation, and the filing fee are required.

Massachusetts

A state pawnbroker license is not required in the State of Massachusetts. However, in order to operate as a pawnbroker, you may be required to get licensed on the local level, as well as you may be required to meet other state requirements. Talk to your local authorities to see what is required before opening your pawnshop.

Maryland

Type of License: Pawnbroker License

Issuing Authority: Department of Labor's Division of Occupational and Professional Licensing

Filing Fees: $100

Other Requirements: Biennial Renewal

Notes: An application, extensive support documentation, and the filing fee are required.

Maine

A state pawnbroker license is not required in the State of Maine. However, in order to operate as a pawnbroker, you may be required to get licensed on the local level, as well as you may be required to meet other state requirements. Talk

to your local authorities to see what is required before opening your pawnshop.

Michigan

A state pawnbroker license is not required in the State of Michigan. However, in order to operate as a pawnbroker, you may be required to get licensed on the local level, as well as you may be required to meet other state requirements. Talk to your local authorities to see what is required before opening your pawnshop.

Minnesota

A state pawnbroker license is not required in the State of Minnesota. However, in order to operate as a pawnbroker, you may be required to get licensed on the local level, as well as you may be required to meet other state requirements. Talk to your local authorities to see what is required before opening your pawnshop.

Missouri

A state pawnbroker license is not required in the State of Missouri. However, in order to operate as a pawnbroker, you may be required to get licensed on the local level, as well as you may be required to meet other state requirements. Talk

to your local authorities to see what is required before opening your pawnshop.

Mississippi

Type of License: Pawnbroker License

Issuing Authority: Department of Banking and Consumer Finance's Pawnshop Division

Filing Fees: $500

Other Requirements: Annual Renewal

Notes: An application, extensive support documentation, and the filing fee are required.

Montana

A state pawnbroker license is not required in the State of Montana. However, in order to operate as a pawnbroker, you may be required to get licensed on the local level, as well as you may be required to meet other state requirements. Talk to your local authorities to see what is required before opening your pawnshop.

North Carolina

A state pawnbroker license is not required in the State of North Carolina. However, in order to operate as a pawnbroker, you may be required to get licensed on the local level, as well as you may be required to meet other state requirements. Talk to your local authorities to see what is required before opening your pawnshop.

North Dakota

A state pawnbroker license is not required in the State of North Dakota. However, in order to operate as a pawnbroker, you may be required to get licensed on the local level, as well as you may be required to meet other state requirements. Talk to your local authorities to see what is required before opening your pawnshop.

Nebraska

A state pawnbroker license is not required in the State of Nebraska. However, in order to operate as a pawnbroker, you may be required to get licensed on the local level, as well as you may be required to meet other state requirements. Talk to your local authorities to see what is required before opening your pawnshop.

New Hampshire

A state pawnbroker license is not required in the State of New Hampshire. However, in order to operate as a pawnbroker, you may be required to get licensed on the local level, as well as you may be required to meet other state requirements. Talk to your local authorities to see what is required before opening your pawnshop.

New Jersey

Type of License: New Jersey Pawnbroker Business License

Issuing Authority: New Jersey Department of Banking and Insurance

Filing Fees: $500

Other Requirements: Biennial Renewal

Notes: An application, extensive support documentation, and the filing fee are required.

New Mexico

A state pawnbroker license is not required in the State of New Mexico. However, in order to operate as a pawnbroker, you may be required to get licensed on the local level, as well as you may be required to meet other state requirements.

Talk to your local authorities to see what is required before opening your pawnshop.

Nevada

A state pawnbroker license is not required in the State of Nevada. However, in order to operate as a pawnbroker, you may be required to get licensed on the local level, as well as you may be required to meet other state requirements. Talk to your local authorities to see what is required before opening your pawnshop.

New York

A state pawnbroker license is not required in the State of New York. However, in order to operate as a pawnbroker, you may be required to get licensed on the local level, as well as you may be required to meet other state requirements. Talk to your local authorities to see what is required before opening your pawnshop.

Ohio

Type of License: Pawnbroker License

Issuing Authority: Department of Commerce's Division of Financial Institutions

Filing Fees: $500 to $800

Other Requirements: Annual Renewal

Notes: An application, extensive support documentation, and the filing fee are required.

Oklahoma

Type of License: Pawnbroker License

Issuing Authority: Department of Consumer Credit

Filing Fees: $240

Other Requirements: Annual Renewal

Notes: An application, extensive support documentation, and the filing fee are required.

Oregon

Type of License: Pawnbroker License

Issuing Authority: Department of Consumer and Business Services

Filing Fees: $500

Other Requirements: Annual Renewal

Notes: An application, extensive support documentation, and the filing fee are required.

Pennsylvania

Type of License: Pawnbroker License

Issuing Authority: Department of Banking and Securities

Filing Fees: $500

Other Requirements: Annual Renewal

Notes: An application, extensive support documentation, and the filing fee are required.

Rhode Island

A state pawnbroker license is not required in the State of Rhode Island. However, in order to operate as a pawnbroker, you may be required to get licensed on the local level, as well as you may be required to meet other state requirements. Talk to your local authorities to see what is required before opening your pawnshop.

South Carolina

Type of License: Pawnbroker License

Issuing Authority: Department of Consumer Affairs

Filing Fees: $275

Other Requirements: Annual Renewal

Notes: An application, extensive support documentation, and the filing fee are required.

South Dakota

A state pawnbroker license is not required in the State of South Dakota. However, in order to operate as a pawnbroker, you may be required to get licensed on the local level, as well as you may be required to meet other state requirements. Talk to your local authorities to see what is required before opening your pawnshop.

Tennessee

A state pawnbroker license is not required in the State of Tennessee. However, in order to operate as a pawnbroker, you may be required to get licensed on the local level, as well as you may be required to meet other state requirements. Talk to your local authorities to see what is required before opening your pawnshop.

Texas

Type of License: Pawnbroker License

Issuing Authority: Office of Consumer Credit Commissioner

Filing Fees: $1,125

Other Requirements: Annual Renewal

Notes: An application, extensive support documentation, and the filing fee are required.

Utah

Type of License: Pawnbroker License

Issuing Authority: Department of Commerce's Division of Consumer Protection

Filing Fees: $300

Other Requirements: Annual Renewal

Notes: An application, extensive support documentation, and the filing fee are required.

Virginia

A state pawnbroker license is not required in the State of Virginia. However, in order to operate as a pawnbroker, you may be required to get licensed on the local level, as well as you may be required to meet other state requirements. Talk to your local authorities to see what is required before opening your pawnshop.

Vermont

A state pawnbroker license is not required in the State of Vermont. However, in order to operate as a pawnbroker, you may be required to get licensed on the local level, as well as you may be required to meet other state requirements. Talk to your local authorities to see what is required before opening your pawnshop.

Washington

A state pawnbroker license is not required in the State of Washington. However, in order to operate as a pawnbroker, you may be required to get licensed on the local level, as well as you may be required to meet other state requirements. Talk to your local authorities to see what is required before opening your pawnshop.

Wisconsin

Type of License: Wisconsin Pawnbroker License

Issuing Authority: Wisconsin Department of Agriculture, Trade and Consumer Protection

Filing Fee: $210

Other Requirements: Annual Renewal

Notes: An application, extensive support documentation, and the filing fee are required.

West Virginia

A state pawnbroker license is not required in the State of West Virginia. However, in order to operate as a pawnbroker, you may be required to get licensed on the local level, as well as you may be required to meet other state requirements. Talk to your local authorities to see what is required before opening your pawnshop.

Wyoming

Type of License: Wyoming Pawnbroker License

Issuing Authority: Wyoming Division of Audit Division of Banking

Filing Fee: $150

Other Requirements: Annual Renewal

Notes: An application, extensive support documentation, and the filing fee are required.

www.ingramcontent.com/pod-product-compliance
Lightning Source LLC
Chambersburg PA
CBHW071407210526
45465CB00001B/293